OXFORD REVISE

AQA GCSE

A CHRISTMAS CAROL

English Literature

COMPLETE REVISION AND PRACTICE

Series Editor: Lyndsay Bawden

Su Fielder

OXFORD
UNIVERSITY PRESS

Contents

Shade in each level of the circle as you feel more confident and ready for your exam.

How to use this book

This book uses a three-step approach to revision: **Knowledge**, **Retrieval**, and **Practice**. It is important that you do all three; they work together to make your revision effective.

Knowledge

Knowledge comes first. Each chapter is divided into **Knowledge Organisers**. These are clear, easy-to-understand, concise summaries of the content that you need to know for your exam. The information is organised to show how one idea flows into the next so you can learn how everything is tied together.

Sample answers and examiner's comments are also provided where appropriate to help you understand what makes a good answer.

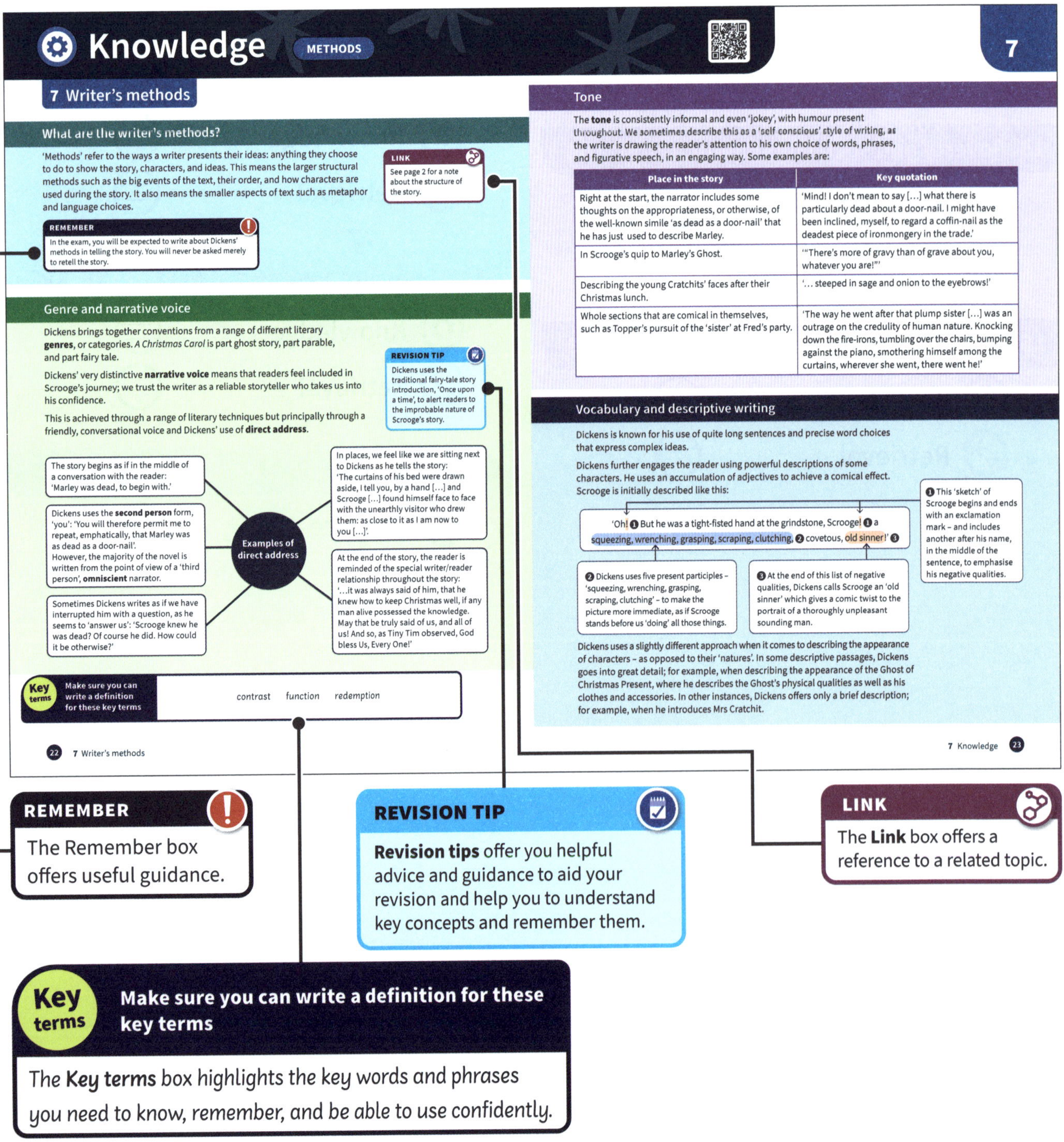

Knowledge METHODS

7

7 Writer's methods

What are the writer's methods?

'Methods' refer to the ways a writer presents their ideas: anything they choose to do to show the story, characters, and ideas. This means the larger structural methods such as the big events of the text, their order, and how characters are used during the story. It also means the smaller aspects of text such as metaphor and language choices.

LINK: See page 2 for a note about the structure of the story.

REMEMBER: In the exam, you will be expected to write about Dickens' methods in telling the story. You will never be asked merely to retell the story.

Genre and narrative voice

Dickens brings together conventions from a range of different literary **genres**, or categories. *A Christmas Carol* is part ghost story, part parable, and part fairy tale.

Dickens' very distinctive **narrative voice** means that readers feel included in Scrooge's journey; we trust the writer as a reliable storyteller who takes us into his confidence.

This is achieved through a range of literary techniques but principally through a friendly, conversational voice and Dickens' use of **direct address**.

REVISION TIP: Dickens uses the traditional fairy-tale story introduction, 'Once upon a time', to alert readers to the improbable nature of Scrooge's story.

Examples of direct address

- The story begins as if in the middle of a conversation with the reader: 'Marley was dead, to begin with.'
- Dickens uses the **second person** form, 'you': 'You will therefore permit me to repeat, emphatically, that Marley was as dead as a door-nail'. However, the majority of the novel is written from the point of view of a 'third person', **omniscient** narrator.
- Sometimes Dickens writes as if we have interrupted him with a question, as he seems to 'answer us': 'Scrooge knew he was dead? Of course he did. How could it be otherwise?'
- In places, we feel like we are sitting next to Dickens as he tells the story: 'The curtains of his bed were drawn aside, I tell you, by a hand […] and Scrooge […] found himself face to face with the unearthly visitor who drew them: as close to it as I am now to you […]'.
- At the end of the story, the reader is reminded of the special writer/reader relationship throughout the story: '…it was always said of him, that he knew how to keep Christmas well, if any man alive possessed the knowledge. May that be truly said of us, and all of us! And so, as Tiny Tim observed, God bless Us, Every One!'

Key terms — Make sure you can write a definition for these key terms: *contrast* *function* *redemption*

22 7 Writer's methods

Tone

The **tone** is consistently informal and even 'jokey', with humour present throughout. We sometimes describe this as a 'self conscious' style of writing, as the writer is drawing the reader's attention to his own choice of words, phrases, and figurative speech, in an engaging way. Some examples are:

Place in the story	Key quotation
Right at the start, the narrator includes some thoughts on the appropriateness, or otherwise, of the well-known simile 'as dead as a door-nail' that he has just used to describe Marley.	'Mind! I don't mean to say […] what there is particularly dead about a door-nail. I might have been inclined, myself, to regard a coffin-nail as the deadest piece of ironmongery in the trade.'
In Scrooge's quip to Marley's Ghost.	'"There's more of gravy than of grave about you, whatever you are!"'
Describing the young Cratchits' faces after their Christmas lunch.	'… steeped in sage and onion to the eyebrows!'
Whole sections that are comical in themselves, such as Topper's pursuit of the 'sister' at Fred's party.	'The way he went after that plump sister […] was an outrage on the credulity of human nature. Knocking down the fire-irons, tumbling over the chairs, bumping against the piano, smothering himself among the curtains, wherever she went, there went he!'

Vocabulary and descriptive writing

Dickens is known for his use of quite long sentences and precise word choices that express complex ideas.

Dickens further engages the reader using powerful descriptions of some characters. He uses an accumulation of adjectives to achieve a comical effect. Scrooge is initially described like this:

'Oh! ❶ But he was a tight-fisted hand at the grindstone, Scrooge! ❶ a squeezing, wrenching, grasping, scraping, clutching, ❷ covetous, old sinner!' ❸

❶ This 'sketch' of Scrooge begins and ends with an exclamation mark – and includes another after his name, in the middle of the sentence, to emphasise his negative qualities.

❷ Dickens uses five present participles – 'squeezing, wrenching, grasping, scraping, clutching' – to make the picture more immediate, as if Scrooge stands before us 'doing' all those things.

❸ At the end of this list of negative qualities, Dickens calls Scrooge an 'old sinner' which gives a comic twist to the portrait of a thoroughly unpleasant sounding man.

Dickens uses a slightly different approach when it comes to describing the appearance of characters – as opposed to their 'natures'. In some descriptive passages, Dickens goes into great detail; for example, when describing the appearance of the Ghost of Christmas Present, where he describes the Ghost's physical qualities as well as his clothes and accessories. In other instances, Dickens offers only a brief description; for example, when he introduces Mrs Cratchit.

7 Knowledge 23

REMEMBER

The Remember box offers useful guidance.

REVISION TIP

Revision tips offer you helpful advice and guidance to aid your revision and help you to understand key concepts and remember them.

LINK

The **Link** box offers a reference to a related topic.

Key terms — Make sure you can write a definition for these key terms

The **Key terms** box highlights the key words and phrases you need to know, remember, and be able to use confidently.

Retrieval

The **Retrieval questions** help you learn and quickly recall the information you've acquired. These are short questions and answers about the Knowledge Organiser content you have just revised. Cover up the answers with some paper and write down as many answers as you can from memory. Check back to the Knowledge Organisers for any you got wrong, then cover the answers and attempt all the questions again until you can answer *all* the questions correctly.

Make sure you revisit the Retrieval questions on different days to help them stick in your memory. You need to write down the answers each time, or say them out loud, for your revision to be effective.

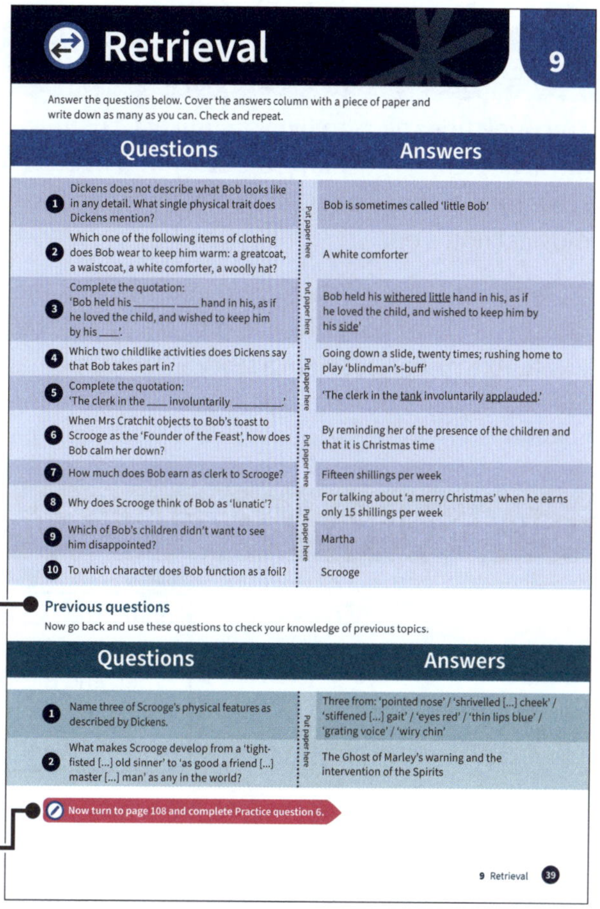

Retrieval

9

Answer the questions below. Cover the answers column with a piece of paper and write down as many as you can. Check and repeat.

	Questions	Answers
1	Dickens does not describe what Bob looks like in any detail. What single physical trait does Dickens mention?	Bob is sometimes called 'little Bob'
2	Which one of the following items of clothing does Bob wear to keep him warm: a greatcoat, a waistcoat, a white comforter, a woolly hat?	A white comforter
3	Complete the quotation: 'Bob held his ________ ____ hand in his, as if he loved the child, and wished to keep him by his ____.'	Bob held his withered little hand in his, as if he loved the child, and wished to keep him by his side'
4	Which two childlike activities does Dickens say that Bob takes part in?	Going down a slide, twenty times; rushing home to play 'blindman's-buff'
5	Complete the quotation: 'The clerk in the ____ involuntarily ________.'	'The clerk in the tank involuntarily applauded.'
6	When Mrs Cratchit objects to Bob's toast to Scrooge as the 'Founder of the Feast', how does Bob calm her down?	By reminding her of the presence of the children and that it is Christmas time
7	How much does Bob earn as clerk to Scrooge?	Fifteen shillings per week
8	Why does Scrooge think of Bob as 'lunatic'?	For talking about 'a merry Christmas' when he earns only 15 shillings per week
9	Which of Bob's children didn't want to see him disappointed?	Martha
10	To which character does Bob function as a foil?	Scrooge

Put paper here

Previous questions

Now go back and use these questions to check your knowledge of previous topics.

	Questions	Answers
1	Name three of Scrooge's physical features as described by Dickens.	Three from: 'pointed nose' / 'shrivelled [...] cheek' / 'stiffened [...] gait' / 'eyes red' / 'thin lips blue' / 'grating voice' / 'wiry chin'
2	What makes Scrooge develop from a 'tight-fisted [...] old sinner' to 'as good a friend [...] master [...] man' as any in the world?	The Ghost of Marley's warning and the intervention of the Spirits

Now turn to page 108 and complete Practice question 6.

9 Retrieval 39

Previous questions

Many Retrieval pages also have some **Retrieval questions** from **previous topics**. Answer these to see if you can remember the content from the earlier sections. If you get the answers wrong, go back and do the Retrieval questions for the earlier topics again.

Practice questions linked to the content you have just been revising are flagged here.

Practice

Once you are confident with the Knowledge Organisers and Retrieval questions, you can move on to the final stage: **Practice**. This can be found at the back of the book.

The **exam-style questions** in this section help you apply all the knowledge you have learned.

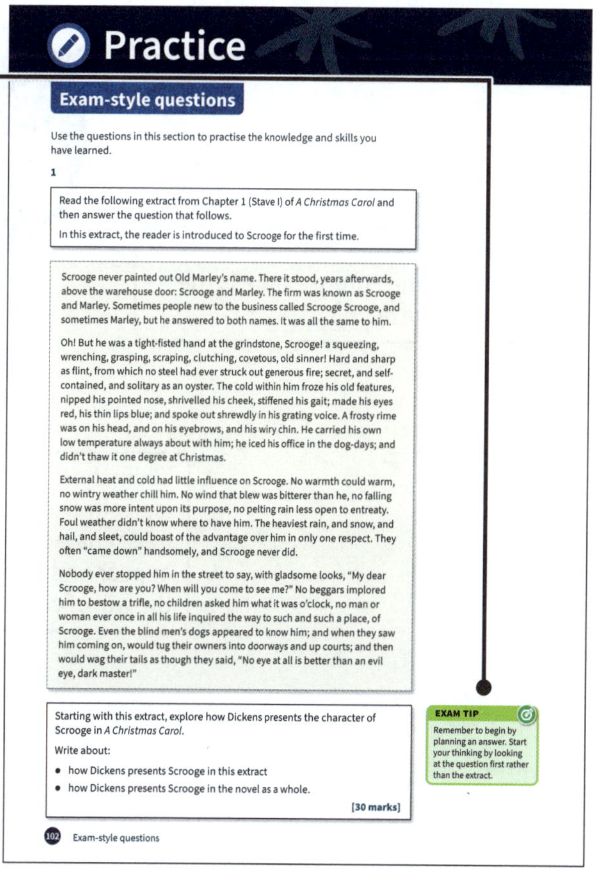

Practice

Exam-style questions

Use the questions in this section to practise the knowledge and skills you have learned.

1

Read the following extract from Chapter 1 (Stave I) of *A Christmas Carol* and then answer the question that follows.

In this extract, the reader is introduced to Scrooge for the first time.

Scrooge never painted out Old Marley's name. There it stood, years afterwards, above the warehouse door: Scrooge and Marley. The firm was known as Scrooge and Marley. Sometimes people new to the business called Scrooge Scrooge, and sometimes Marley, but he answered to both names. It was all the same to him.

Oh! But he was a tight-fisted hand at the grindstone, Scrooge! a squeezing, wrenching, grasping, scraping, clutching, covetous, old sinner! Hard and sharp as flint, from which no steel had ever struck out generous fire; secret, and self-contained, and solitary as an oyster. The cold within him froze his old features, nipped his pointed nose, shrivelled his cheek, stiffened his gait; made his eyes red, his thin lips blue; and spoke out shrewdly in his grating voice. A frosty rime was on his head, and on his eyebrows, and his wiry chin. He carried his own low temperature always about with him; he iced his office in the dog-days; and didn't thaw it one degree at Christmas.

External heat and cold had little influence on Scrooge. No warmth could warm, no wintry weather chill him. No wind that blew was bitterer than he, no falling snow was more intent upon its purpose, no pelting rain less open to entreaty. Foul weather didn't know where to have him. The heaviest rain, and snow, and hail, and sleet, could boast of the advantage over him in only one respect. They often "came down" handsomely, and Scrooge never did.

Nobody ever stopped him in the street to say, with gladsome looks, "My dear Scrooge, how are you? When will you come to see me?" No beggars implored him to bestow a trifle, no children asked him what it was o'clock, no man or woman ever once in all his life inquired the way to such and such a place, of Scrooge. Even the blind men's dogs appeared to know him; and when they saw him coming on, would tug their owners into doorways and up courts; and then would wag their tails as though they said, "No eye at all is better than an evil eye, dark master!"

Starting with this extract, explore how Dickens presents the character of Scrooge in *A Christmas Carol*.

Write about:

- how Dickens presents Scrooge in this extract
- how Dickens presents Scrooge in the novel as a whole.

[30 marks]

EXAM TIP

Remember to begin by planning an answer. Start your thinking by looking at the question first rather than the extract.

102 Exam-style questions

EXAM TIP

Exam tips show you how to interpret the questions, provide guidance on how to answer them, and give advice on how to secure as many marks as possible. Guidance is also offered on how to approach different command words.

Answers and Glossary

You can scan the QR codes at any time to access sample answers and mark schemes for the exam-style questions, a glossary containing definitions of the key terms, as well as further revision support, or go to go.oup.com/OR/GCSE/A/EngLit/Christmas

Knowledge PLOT

1 Structure and summary

The structure of *A Christmas Carol*

The book title refers to hymns sung at Christmas time, and Dickens continues this musical theme by dividing the story into five 'staves', not chapters, to form the **structure** of the book. A 'stave' refers to the five lines used by composers to write musical notes on.

A Christmas Carol is categorised as a 'novella', meaning a short novel. It is part ghost story, part **parable**, and part fairy tale. The main character, Scrooge, learns a valuable moral lesson in a story where supernatural elements interfere in the life of a flawed human, leading to a happy ending.

Time and place in *A Christmas Carol*

REVISION TIP

Try to keep a note of *when* and *where* each piece of action occurs.

Time and place

- Unlike the rest of the staves, the action in Stave I takes place in chronological order, and the movement of the living characters, from one place to another, happens 'naturally'.
- Both 'time' and 'place' are important in this story.
- Church bells and city clocks, as well as Scrooge's own pocket watch, accurately mark the time until the ghost of Marley and the Spirits make their entrance. After this, time moves erratically for Scrooge.
- While the action generally shifts logically from one place to another for most characters, for Scrooge, 'places' appear and disappear, according to the will of each Spirit.
- The Spirits represent the Present, the Past, and the Future – time is the medium for the action.
- References to time and place are vital in allowing the reader to imagine the different settings of the story.

2 Stave I

Key ideas

- Three sets of 'visitors' arrive to see Scrooge; he receives them in his 'counting-house', ironically surrounded by evidence of his financial security. Dickens uses the contrast between the rooms where Scrooge and Bob work to convey his ideas about social inequality.
- Each has an invitation or 'request' to make of Scrooge; they are all denied or refused by mean-spirited Scrooge.
- Bob, though poor, can take pleasure in the ice and a game with his family. His joy despite his poverty conveys Dickens' key theme of the importance of family.
- Scrooge, though rich, has no such joy, having only his 'banker's-book' for company. Scrooge's financial security contrasts with Bob's poverty, illustrating Dickens' key theme of social inequality.
- Scrooge returns home alone. He is shocked by the recognition that, though Marley drags around the chain he 'forged in life', Scrooge's own chain, seven years on from Marley's death, will be even more of a 'ponderous chain'.
- Marley's harrowing experience of the afterlife persuades Scrooge that his soul is in danger. He falls asleep unable to sum up his experience of Marley and the other ghostly forms as 'humbug'. This is the start of Scrooge's journey towards redemption, one of the key ideas of the story.

REMEMBER !

The three sets of visitors each represent an aspect of Christmas, and each is dismissed by Scrooge with increasing levels of rudeness.

Key events

- On Christmas Eve, Ebenezer Scrooge works in his office with his clerk, Bob Cratchit.
- Scrooge's nephew, Fred, comes to invite him for Christmas dinner. Scrooge ungraciously declines the invitation. Scrooge and Fred disagree about the significance of Christmas as a special time of year.
- Fred leaves and two 'portly gentlemen' arrive, seeking a donation to help the poor over Christmas. Scrooge refuses to contribute.
- An unnamed boy attempts to sing a carol for Scrooge but is scared away by him.
- At the end of the day, Scrooge warns Bob Cratchit to arrive early for work on the day after Christmas.
- Scrooge goes home, but his door knocker mysteriously turns into the face of his old business partner, Jacob Marley, who has been dead for exactly seven years.
- Later, Scrooge is shocked when confronted by the ghost of Jacob Marley, who is dragging a long chain made up of things related to money.
- Marley has come to warn Scrooge to change his selfish and greedy ways to avoid the fate that he himself is suffering, as the ghost of a man whose life was devoted to making money.
- Marley tells Scrooge that he will be haunted by three Spirits who will offer Scrooge the chance to take a new path in life that will lead to happiness rather than regret.

Knowledge PLOT

2 Stave I

Key moments

Narrative/Character/Action	Significance	Key quotation
Stave I is entitled 'Marley's Ghost'.	Readers expect something spooky to happen.	'Marley was dead, to begin with.'
Scrooge is described negatively, as 'hard', 'sharp', and 'cold'; Fred's description as 'warm' is positive.	Scrooge and Fred are shown to be opposites. Scrooge's contempt and Fred's care for others show on their faces.	'The cold within him froze his old features…' '…he was all in a glow; his face was ruddy and handsome; his eyes sparkled…'
Scrooge refuses Fred's invitation and threatens to fire Bob.	Scrooge's meanness is emphasised since Dickens presents Christmas as a time for love and charity to others, a key idea in the story.	'"Christmas a humbug, uncle!" said Scrooge's nephew. "You don't mean that, I am sure?" "I do," said Scrooge.'
The two 'portly gentlemen' do not persuade Scrooge to part with his money.	Scrooge shows a lack of humanity in his attitude to the poor, asking if there are still prisons and workhouses to shelter them. When told 'many would rather die' than go there, Scrooge is heartless in his reply. Dickens uses the portly gentlemen to convey his own views on the poor and on social inequality.	'"If they would rather die," said Scrooge, "they had better do it, and decrease the surplus population."'

Narrative/Character/Action	Significance	Key quotation
Scrooge begrudgingly allows Bob a day off to celebrate Christmas.	Even though it occurs only once a year, Scrooge tries to make Bob feel guilty about the holiday. Throughout the story, Christmas is portrayed as time of goodwill and charity and is an important theme of the story.	'"A poor excuse for picking a man's pocket every twenty-fifth of December!"'
Scrooge is perplexed when his door knocker morphs into the face of Jacob Marley; but he is not terrified.	Even when confronted by the ghost of Marley, he is still prepared to think the vision may be caused by indigestion.	'"You don't believe in me," […]' '"I don't", said Scrooge. […] "You may be an undigested bit of beef, a blot of mustard, a crumb of cheese […]"'
When Marley begins making an appalling noise, Scrooge is forced to pay attention.	Scrooge finally accepts that Marley has returned to help him to understand what his proper business should be.	'"Mankind was my business […] charity, mercy, forbearance, and benevolence were, all, my business."'
Scrooge is shocked by Marley's suffering and the misery of the phantoms.	Scrooge, who cared for none but himself, begins his journey towards becoming a part of humanity. This idea of redemption is one of the key themes Dickens explores in the story.	'The misery with them all was, clearly, that they sought to interfere, for good, in human matters, and had lost the power for ever.'

REVISION TIP

Revise the characters' names and relationships so that you don't confuse them in the exam.

Key terms Make sure you can write a definition for these key terms

parable *structure*

Retrieval

Answer the questions below. Cover the answers column with a piece of paper and write down as many as you can. Check and repeat.

	Questions	Answers
1	Why does Dickens call the different parts of the story 'staves'?	Because he is continuing the musical theme introduced in the title, *A Christmas Carol*
2	What happens when the unnamed boy attempts to sing a carol for Scrooge?	Scrooge scares him away
3	What invitation does Fred extend to his Uncle Scrooge?	To join him for Christmas dinner
4	The 'portly gentlemen' who visit Scrooge have come for what purpose?	To ask him to donate money to help the poor and destitute at Christmas
5	What three items would Scrooge's donation help to provide for the poor?	Meat; drink; warmth
6	Name two items that make up the chains dragged by the Ghost of Marley.	Two from: cashboxes / keys / padlocks / financial ledgers
7	What part of the offices does Scrooge sit in?	The counting-house
8	Name two adjectives used to describe Scrooge.	Two from: 'hard' / 'sharp' / 'cold'
9	Scrooge asks the 'portly gentlemen' whether two public institutions, open to the poor and destitute, are still in operation: name each of them.	Prisons; workhouses
10	Complete the quotation: '"If they would rather die," said Scrooge, "they had better do it, and decrease the _______ _______."'	'"If they would rather die," said Scrooge, "they had better do it, and decrease the surplus population."'
11	Complete the quotation: '"A poor excuse for _______ _______ _______ _______ every twenty-fifth of December!"'	'"A poor excuse for picking a man's pocket every twenty-fifth of December!"'
12	Scrooge is capable of being humorous even before his 'transformation'; complete the quotation as he speaks to Marley: '"There's more of _______ _______ _______ _______ about you, whatever you are!"'	'"There's more of gravy than of grave about you, whatever you are!"'

Now turn to page 102 and complete Practice question 1.

3 Stave II

Key ideas

- Scrooge wakes to finds time disrupted – the first of many occasions where the Spirits 'disorder' time. Time is the medium that Dickens uses to reflect upon what Scrooge was like in his youth, his middle years, and how he was reclaimed.
- Scrooge's lonely childhood may have contributed to his meanness. The memory of his boyhood prompts Scrooge to regret his treatment of the unnamed boy. Dickens is using the young Scrooge to start to show that Scrooge can change and be saved.
- Scrooge remembers the joy that Fezziwig's generosity brought to him and his fellow workers. Dickens shows that Christmas spirit can bring people together joyfully.
- Scrooge finds it 'torture' to see Belle end their engagement due to his love of money. Dickens shows that Scrooge's greed has denied him love and joy.
- Seeing Belle's happy family, Scrooge mourns the loss of what might have been. Scrooge is distressed to realise that his greed has cost him a family, and Dickens shows how this might have brought him happiness.

REMEMBER

The terms 'Spirit', 'Ghost', and sometimes 'Phantom' are used interchangeably in the story.

Key events

- Scrooge is woken by the church clock and wonders if Marley's Ghost was a dream. At the strike of 1:00am, the Ghost of Christmas Past appears.
- The Ghost begins Scrooge's tour of Christmases past, leading him to the place where he grew up.
- Scrooge is delighted to see familiar landmarks and faces, and to hear boys that he had known, wishing one another a Merry Christmas.
- The Ghost takes Scrooge to see his young self sitting alone at Christmas, absorbed in reading. Seeing the fictional characters he loved as a child, Scrooge regrets his behaviour to the unnamed boy.
- Scrooge's sister, Fan, arrives. The Ghost reminds Scrooge of Fan's early death, and that Fred is her son.
- Scrooge relives Fezziwig's Christmas party when he was an apprentice, which makes him wish he might 'say a word or two' to his clerk.
- The next vision shows Scrooge in his twenties. His fiancée, Belle, releases him from their engagement, knowing that Scrooge puts money above her.
- Despite Scrooge's pleas to stop, the Ghost forces him to see what he has lost. Scrooge sees Belle, with her children and kindly husband. Scrooge hears them laugh at him for working while Marley is on his deathbed.
- Scrooge begs to be removed and attempts, but fails, to extinguish the light of the Spirit.

REVISION TIP

Make a note of each moment where Scrooge's reaction to what the Spirits have shown him brings him closer to being a changed man.

Knowledge PLOT

3 Stave II

Key moments

Narrative/Character/Action	Significance	Key quotation
Scrooge is afraid of *physical* harm, if he falls, as the Spirit leads him to the window.	He is on the brink of *spiritual* change, which begins with the Spirit touching him on his heart. Dickens shows that Scrooge should be more concerned with the condition of his soul than his body.	'"Bear but a touch of my hand *there*," said the Spirit, laying it upon his heart, "and you shall be upheld in more than this!"'
As they pass through the wall to the country road, the mist and darkness vanish.	The Spirit's touch dispels the darkness, restoring Scrooge's clearer sight of the world.	'He was conscious of […] a thousand thoughts, and hopes, and joys, and cares long, long forgotten!'
The Spirit shows Scrooge his younger self, miserable and abandoned at Christmas.	The vision makes Scrooge feel compassion. Dickens is using the medium of time to show the characters development, a key theme throughout the story.	'a lonely boy was reading near a feeble fire; and Scrooge sat down […] and wept to see his poor forgotten self'
Scrooge enjoys Fezziwig's Christmas party, and he appreciates the hospitality shown by Mr and Mrs Fezziwig to the whole workforce.	This reminds Scrooge of his own responsibility as an employer. This illustrates Dickens' theme of social inequality, conveying his beliefs that those with wealth and influence should help people rather than enriching themselves at the cost of others.	'"He has the power to […] make our service light or burdensome; a pleasure or a toil."' '"I should like to be able to say a word or two to my clerk just now."'
The Spirit dampens Scrooge's new-found zest by showing him the scene where Belle releases him from their engagement.	Scrooge sees the idealistic young man he once was, offering some hope for his eventual redemption and revival of his earlier qualities.	'"I have seen your nobler aspirations fall off one by one, until the master-passion, Gain, engrosses you."'
The recollection of Belle's final words to him are agony to Scrooge; he regrets the missed opportunity to reassure Belle of her importance to him.	At each successive vision, Scrooge's heart softens a little more. He is beginning the journey towards his salvation.	'"May you be happy in the life you have chosen!"' '"No more!" cried Scrooge. "No more! I don't wish to see it."'
The final vision in this stave does not include Scrooge. While observing Belle's joyous family Christmas, he hears mention of his name.	Scrooge is horrified to learn how insignificant he has become to Belle, and that, to Belle and her husband, he is a figure of fun. Belle and her family represent the themes of family and Christmas spirit as they celebrate together.	'"I saw an old friend of yours […]"' '"Mr. Scrooge it was […] and there he sat alone. Quite alone in the world, I do believe."'

Sight, sound, and touch in Staves I and II

Sights, sounds, touch

- Scrooge is surrounded by thick 'fog and darkness' as he makes his way home at the end of Stave I.
- In Stave I, Scrooge sees Marley's Ghost float out 'upon the bleak, dark night', suggesting the **benighted** state of Scrooge before the Spirits visit.
- In Stave II, when Scrooge first sees the Ghost of Christmas Past, the 'strangest thing about it' is the 'bright clear jet of light' that springs from the crown of its head, the light flooding Scrooge's darkness.
- In Stave II, Scrooge listens attentively to the chiming of the bells, so that his senses of sight and sound are both engaged.
- Marley's visit and the touch of the Ghost of Christmas Past spark off a new willingness in Scrooge to look, hear, feel, and learn from his mistakes by the end of Stave II.
- At the beginning of Stave II, Scrooge wakes to darkness but tries to 'pierce the darkness with his ferret eyes, when the chimes of a neighbouring church struck the four quarters'. Dickens may be suggesting that Scrooge is **metaphorically** in darkness about the real meaning of Christmas and of life itself.

REVISION TIP

Try to keep a note of the sights, sounds and feelings that Scrooge experiences when in the company of each of the Ghosts of Christmas.

Key terms Make sure you can write a definition for these key terms

benighted *metaphorically*

Retrieval

Answer the questions below. Cover the answers column with a piece of paper and write down as many as you can. Check and repeat.

	Questions	Answers
1	When Scrooge wakes up to the striking church clock, what does he think might have happened?	That his experience with the Ghost of Marley was a dream
2	What two things happen at the stroke of 1:00am?	Light flashes up in Scrooge's room; the curtains around Scrooge's bed are pulled aside by a strange figure – the Ghost of Christmas Past
3	When Scrooge remembers the unhappiness of his own boyhood, what regret does he voice to the Ghost of Christmas Past?	Not giving the unnamed boy something for his carol
4	Name two senses that Dickens refers to once the Ghost of Christmas Past arrives.	Two from: sight / sound / touch
5	What is the 'strangest thing' about the appearance of the Ghost of Christmas Past?	The 'bright clear jet of light' that springs from the crown of his head
6	Complete the quotation: 'a lonely boy was reading near a feeble fire; and Scrooge sat down […] and wept to see his _______ _______ _______'.	'a lonely boy was reading near a feeble fire; and Scrooge sat down […] and wept to see his poor forgotten self'.
7	Why does Belle release Scrooge from their engagement?	Because he has changed towards her
8	What does Belle say has become Scrooge's 'master-passion'?	Gain
9	What has Scrooge become in the eyes of Belle and her husband?	A figure of fun

Put paper here

Previous questions

Now go back and use these questions to check your knowledge of previous topics.

	Questions	Answers
1	The 'portly gentlemen' who visit Scrooge have come for what purpose?	To ask him to donate money to help the poor and destitute at Christmas
2	What three items would Scrooge's donation help to provide for the poor?	Meat; drink; warmth

Put paper here

Now turn to page 107 and complete Practice question 5.

4 Stave III

Key ideas

- Scrooge sees the Ghost of Christmas Present surrounded by all sorts of Christmas paraphernalia that he usually describes as 'humbug'. The theme of Christmas spirit embodies the qualities of kindness, forgiveness, and charity. Dickens shows that Scrooge has rejected these qualities, just as he has rejected the paraphernalia of Christmas. Dickens uses motifs of warmth, light, and brightness to convey the idea of Christmas spirit.
- Scrooge watches the Cratchit family enjoy a happy but modest celebration of Christmas. Scrooge, 'with an interest he had never felt before' asks if 'Tiny Tim will live'. The Cratchits are a happy family, representing Dickens' ideas around the importance of family and what Scrooge has given up through his own greed.
- The various locations show Scrooge how **universally** Christmas is celebrated: 'every man […], had had a kinder word for another on that day […] and had shared […] in its festivities; and had remembered those he cared for at a distance, and had known that they delighted to remember him.' Dickens' shows that Christmas is as much a state of mind as a time of year, representing goodness and kindness.
- Scrooge enjoys Fred's Christmas party. When his niece plays a tune, beloved by his sister, Fan, 'he softened more and more…'
- Fred drinks to his health and Scrooge would have 'thanked them in an inaudible speech, if the Ghost had given him time'. Dickens shows that the spirit of Christmas is powerful and has a significant impact on Scrooge.
- 'Much they saw, and far they went, and many homes they visited, but always with a happy end.'
- Scrooge visits sick beds, almshouses, hospitals, and jails and everywhere the Spirit goes, 'he left his blessing, and taught Scrooge his **precepts**.'
- Dickens shows Scrooge witnessing celebrations in many different places, reflecting the universality of Christmas spirit.
- Scrooge is ashamed when presented with 'Ignorance' and 'Want', and is reminded of his earlier indifference to the sufferings of others. The children are a stark reminder of Dickens' key themes of social inequality and poverty.
- A new stage in Scrooge's journey is about to begin.

Key events

- Scrooge wakes at 1:00am to find the adjoining room transformed into a kind of Christmas grotto with the Ghost of Christmas Present seated upon a throne of festive food and drink.
- Scrooge willingly offers to go with the Ghost.
- The first vision is Bob Cratchit's home; Scrooge sees how much the family love and care for one another and notes that despite being poor, the Cratchits are contented.

REVISION TIP

The first two Spirits set Scrooge on his path to avoid Marley's fate, and all the visions he sees take him further along this path.

Knowledge PLOT

4 Stave III

- Scrooge asks the Ghost if Tiny Tim will live. Scrooge is told that Tim will die without some future intervention.
- Mrs Cratchit objects to Bob drinking a toast to Scrooge – the 'Founder of the Feast' – but finally agrees at Bob's insistence.
- The Ghost takes Scrooge to visit a coal mine, a lighthouse, and a ship at sea, where they see people happily celebrating Christmas in their own ways.
- The last visit is to a Christmas party at the home of Scrooge's nephew, Fred.
- Scrooge hears Fred, his wife, and friends talking and laughing about Scrooge and his view that Christmas is a 'humbug'.
- Fred's determination to wish Scrooge well causes Scrooge to be 'light of heart' and willing to return their toast but he is whisked away by the Spirit.
- The Ghost of Christmas Present reveals two 'wretched' children, concealed beneath his robes, representing 'Ignorance' and 'Want'.
- Scrooge asks what refuge or resource there may be for them. The Spirit turns on Scrooge with his own heartless words – prisons, workhouses.
- As the clock strikes 12:00 am the Ghost of Christmas Present vanishes. Scrooge remembers Marley's prediction and looks up to see a 'solemn Phantom'.

Key moments

Narrative/Character/Action	Significance	Key quotation
The Ghost of Christmas Present is a welcoming, genial Spirit; consistently cheery in manner.	Scrooge immediately trusts his new guide and is more open with him, showing his spiritual progress.	'"Spirit [...] conduct me where you will. I went forth last night on compulsion, and I learnt a lesson which is working now. To-night, if you have aught to teach me, let me profit by it."'
The Spirit carries a torch from which he sprinkles 'incense' on ordinary folk to improve their lives.	This Ghost **personifies** good will, charity, and love, qualities represented by Christmas spirit throughout the story. He tells Scrooge that he mostly chooses to sprinkle 'incense' on the dinners of the poor, who need it most, conveying Dickens' views on the need for social justice and help for the poor.	'"Would it apply to any kind of dinner on this day?" asked Scrooge. '"To any kindly given. To a poor one most." '"Why to a poor one most?" asked Scrooge. '"Because it needs it most."'

Narrative/Character/Action	Significance	Key quotation
Scrooge shows concern for Tiny Tim, and the Spirit quotes back at Scrooge his previous opinion about 'the surplus population'.	The Spirit teaches Scrooge **humility**. Dickens uses Tiny Tim to represent victims of a society that favours the wealthy and makes inadequate provision for the poor.	'"Will you decide what men shall live, what men shall die? It may be, that in the sight of Heaven, you are more worthless and less fit to live than millions like this poor man's child."'
Bob proposes a toast to Scrooge – the rest of the family copy reluctantly.	Scrooge learns the family's poor opinion of him.	'Scrooge was the Ogre of the family. The mention of his name cast a dark shadow on the party'
Scrooge enjoys the fun and music at Fred's home, finding joy in Fred's toast.	The Spirit has taught Scrooge to appreciate the meaning of Christmas, and how Christmas spirit can bring people together.	'Scrooge had imperceptibly become so [. . .] light of heart'
The Ghost of Christmas Present's visit ends sombrely with the revelation of the dangers of Want and Ignorance.	Scrooge is alerted to his wider role in the community to help those worse off than himself. This conveys Dickens' view regarding social responsibility and the need to help others.	'"This boy is Ignorance. This girl is Want. Beware them both"'

Minor characters

In *A Christmas Carol*, Dickens weaves multiple minor characters into the plot, supporting the themes of the novel and enlarging the reader's understanding of Scrooge's journey to become a better man.

In Stave III, Dickens introduces minor characters, to show how Christmas is celebrated universally, and to support his ideas about Christmas..

Atmosphere

Some create the special atmosphere of Christmas, for example: people shovelling snow were 'full of glee'; others are 'flocking through the streets in their best clothes'. Dickens shows Christmas to be a time of joy and harmony.

Christmas shopping

Shopkeepers convey the sense of busy Christmas. Through the story, Dickens conveys the idea that the abundance of Christmas should be shared with the poor on every day of the year.

Christmas spirit

Others emphasise the universality of the Christmas spirit: in the miners' hut a man was 'singing them a Christmas song'; lighthouse men 'wished each other Merry Christmas'; all those on the ship 'hummed a Christmas tune'. Dickens shows that Christmas spirit can be found in any circumstances and should be embodied all year round.

Key terms Make sure you can write a definition for these key terms

humility *personify* *precept* *universally*

Retrieval

Answer the questions below. Cover the answers column with a piece of paper and write down as many as you can. Check and repeat.

	Questions	Answers
1	When Scrooge follows the light into the adjoining room, he finds the Ghost of Christmas Present sitting on what?	A 'throne' of festive food and drink
2	Why does Scrooge go willingly with the Ghost of Christmas Present?	Because he has learned from the last Spirit's visit and expects the visit will do him good
3	What does Scrooge ask the Spirit about Tiny Tim?	If the boy will live
4	When Bob proposes a toast to Scrooge, what does he describe him as? Complete the quotation: '_____ of the _____'.	'<u>Founder</u> of the <u>Feast</u>'.
5	The Ghost takes Scrooge to visit different places, to show him how Christmas is observed far and wide: name two of these places.	Two from: a coal mine / a lighthouse / a ship / sickbeds / jails / hospitals / almshouses
6	At Fred's party, what happens to Scrooge when he hears a tune loved by his sister, Fan?	He softens ('he softened more and more…')
7	Name two qualities that the Ghost of Christmas Present personifies.	Two from: good will / charity / love
8	How do the Cratchit family actually view Scrooge?	As the 'Ogre' of the family
9	What do the 'wretched' children shown by the Spirit represent?	Want and Ignorance

Put paper here

Previous questions

Now go back and use these questions to check your knowledge of previous topics.

	Questions	Answers
1	When Scrooge wakes up to the striking church clock, what does he think might have happened?	That his experience with the Ghost of Marley was a dream
2	Which two things happen at the stroke of 1:00am?	Light flashes up in Scrooge's room and the curtains around Scrooge's bed are pulled aside by the Ghost of Christmas Past
3	What is the 'strangest thing' about the appearance of the Ghost of Christmas Past?	The 'bright clear jet of light' that springs from the crown of his head

Put paper here

Now turn to page 106 and complete Practice question 4.

5 Stave IV

Key ideas

- The third Spirit 'seemed to scatter gloom and mystery' and is a different kind of Spirit, filling Scrooge with dread.
- The Spirit signals to Scrooge to listen to two sets of businessmen talking about a man who has just died. Dickens is employing **irony**, as the reader knows that they are discussing Scrooge (referred to by one as 'old Scratch') but Scrooge is unaware of this and is shocked by their unfeeling tone.
- Scrooge hears the three thieves insult the dead man they have stolen from. One calls him 'a wicked old screw'. All agree they were able to rob him because he had 'frightened every one away from him when he was alive', so that he died alone. Dickens uses the physical appearance of the characters to convey his ideas about the ugliness of greed. The characters' dialogue presents the life-sapping quality of pursuing money for money's sake.
- Scrooge thinks about the dead man: '"if this man could be raised up now, what would be his [...] thoughts? **Avarice**, hard-dealing, griping cares? They have brought him to a rich end, truly!"' Scrooge has learned another lesson about the misery brought by greed.
- Scrooge did not expect the emotion caused by the man's death to be 'pleasure'. He is desperate to see some show of 'tenderness'. His heart continues to soften.
- Scrooge sees the Cratchits' tender feelings for the loss of Tiny Tim. He hears Bob saying how Fred comforted him and offered help: '"It really seemed as if he had known our Tiny Tim, and felt with us."' At the start of the story, Scrooge was solitary and had no friends. Dickens shows that he is beginning to see the value of family and friendship.
- The Spirit ignores Scrooge's wish to see himself 'in days to come', pointing him to a grave headstone with his name. Scrooge's promise to be a better man touches even the Phantom. The Spirits have fulfilled their mission. Dickens shows that Scrooge is a changed man; he has realised the value of kindness.

REVISION TIP

The unnamed characters and the people in the shop are minor characters supporting Dickens' portrayal of Scrooge.

Knowledge PLOT

5 Stave IV

Key events

- The Ghost of Christmas Yet to Come is a silent and ominous 'Phantom'. It simply points the way, to the heart of the city, where Scrooge overhears businessmen discussing someone's death and making jokes.
- The Phantom takes Scrooge to a sordid shop, trading in stolen goods. Scrooge watches as a laundress, a charwoman and an undertaker arrive to sell their ill-gotten gains.
- All three have robbed a man as he lay dead. Each stole paltry items, such as sleeve-buttons, sheets and towels, sugar-tongs, and silver teaspoons. One stole the bed-curtains that hung around his deathbed. They make coarse and cruel jokes about the deceased and are pleased to make a few shillings at his expense.
- Scrooge is horrified to find himself in the bedroom of the dead man whose corpse is simply covered in a ragged sheet.
- Scrooge asks the Phantom to show him any person who 'feels emotion caused by this man's death'. He is transported to a home where a young mother and father rejoice at the news of the man's death, since they owed him money, and only his death prevented them from possibly having to go to a **debtors' prison**.
- Seeing that the emotion connected with this death was pleasure, Scrooge begs the Spirit to take him where there is 'some tenderness connected with a death'.
- The Phantom takes him back to the home of the Cratchits, where the family is mourning the death of Tiny Tim.
- Scrooge asks a final favour of the Phantom, to tell him who the man is that nobody seemed to care for in death. The Phantom shows him a headstone on a grave in an overgrown plot marked 'Ebenezer Scrooge'.
- Scrooge makes a promise to the Spirit: to honour Christmas all the year, and never to forget the lessons he has learned of all three Spirits, if he is given the chance to live 'an altered life'.
- The Phantom's 'hood and dress' shrinks and collapses before his eyes and turns into a bedpost. Scrooge is back in his own bed.

Key terms **Make sure you can write a definition for these key terms**

avarice *debtors' prison* *irony*

Key moments

Narrative/Character/Action	Significance	Key quotation
The Ghost of Christmas Yet to Come – the Phantom – is a silent and forbidding Spirit who communicates through pointing and through slight movements of his head and hand.	Though Scrooge is becoming quite used to his ghostly guides and determined to benefit from their teachings the Phantom makes him very uncomfortable.	'Scrooge felt an uncertain horror, to know that behind the dusky shroud, there were ghostly eyes intently fixed upon him, while he […] could see nothing but a spectral hand and one great heap of black.'
Scrooge keeps looking for a future vision of himself. Instead the Phantom shows his grim future if he does not change his ways.	He will be: • disrespected and laughed at by his peers in the city • despised by his own staff who rob him as he lies dead • wished dead by those who owe him money. Dickens presents a grim future for Scrooge if he continues to be greedy and unkind to others.	'... why wasn't he natural in his lifetime? If he had been, he'd have had somebody to look after him when he was struck with Death, instead of lying gasping out his last there, alone by himself.'
When he hears the heartless words universally spoken about the 'dead man', Scrooge is determined to complete his transformation.	The Phantom teaches Scrooge that his current path can only lead to a lonely death. Scrooge is ready to change conveying Dickens' key idea of redemption.	'"I will honour Christmas in my heart, and try to keep it all the year. […] The Spirits […] shall strive within me. I will not shut out the lessons that they teach."'

Atmosphere in Staves I to IV

Content of each stave is reflected in the atmosphere

Stave I:
- Introduction to Scrooge and his miserly ways: cold and dark atmosphere
- Sudden, unexpected appearance of the Ghost of Marley: 'spooky' atmosphere, with anticipation for what is to come

Stave II:
Scrooge is conducted on his tour of Christmases 'past': mainly nostalgic atmosphere

Stave III:
The Ghost of Christmas Present is jovial and encourages Scrooge in his pleasant mood as he watches Fred's party, for example: happier, jollier atmosphere

Stave IV:
- The Phantom is silent and ominous, the visions often show people at their worst sombre in atmosphere, filling Scrooge with fear and dread.
- The goodness of the Cratchits, even in grief: this is the only time with a 'heart-warming' atmosphere

REVISION TIP

When you are re-reading sections of the novel, make notes about the atmosphere of each section of the plot.

LINK

Look closely at Methods on pages 22–27 where Dickens' creation of atmosphere is addressed in more detail.

Retrieval

Answer the questions below. Cover the answers column with a piece of paper and write down as many as you can. Check and repeat.

	Questions	Answers
1	How does the Phantom communicate with Scrooge?	Through pointing and slight movements of his head and hand
2	Scrooge asks the Phantom to show him any person who 'feels emotion caused by this man's death'. Who does the Phantom show him and what emotion is felt at the news of his death?	The young mother and/or the young father, who feel pleasure at his death, as they owed him money
3	Where does the Phantom take Scrooge when he asks to be shown some 'tenderness' connected to a death?	To the Cratchits' home where Tiny Tim is being mourned
4	Complete the quotation: unlike the first two spirits who each appeared surrounded by light the Phantom, 'seemed to scatter _____ _____ _____'.	'seemed to scatter gloom and mystery'.
5	What nickname does one of the wealthy businessmen use when referring to Scrooge?	Old Scratch
6	Name two of the characters in the sordid shop where Scrooge's stolen possessions are being traded.	Two from: Old Joe / a laundress / a charwoman / an undertaker
7	How did the three thieves explain why it was so easy to steal from the dead man?	They say "He frightened every one away from him when he was alive" so he died alone, with nobody to protect his property
8	Complete the quotation: '"if this man could be raised up now, what would be his [...] thoughts? _____, _____-_____, _____ _____? They have brought him to a rich end, truly!"'	'"if this man could be raised up now, what would be his [...] thoughts? Avarice, hard-dealing, griping cares? They have brought him to a rich end, truly!"'
9	How is Scrooge affected by hearing the dead man universally spoken ill of and laughed at?	He is determined to complete his transformation

Previous questions

Now go back and use these questions to check your knowledge of previous topics.

	Questions	Answers
1	What does Scrooge ask the Spirit about Tiny Tim?	If the boy will live
2	How do the Cratchit family actually view Scrooge?	As the 'Ogre' of the family

Now turn to page 114 and complete Practice question 11.

6 Stave V

Key ideas

- Scrooge is generous with the unknown boy who fetches the poulterer to deliver a turkey to Bob Cratchit. Scrooge has come to see that the meaning of Christmas spirit is goodwill, kindness and helping others, conveying a key message of the story.
- Scrooge gives money to the portly gentleman, and his new attitude to giving conveys Dickens' views on social responsibility and helping others.
- Dickens shows that Scrooge has realised the importance of family through his reconciliation with Fred.
- Scrooge carries out his intention to become a model employer, like Mr Fezziwig. Dickens is showing the importance of trying to rectify social inequality and helping others rather than hoarding wealth.
- Redemption is a key idea in the story, and Scrooge is determined to become a force of good in the world and turn his back on his miserly and unsympathetic ways of living.

LINK

Marley is mentioned at the start of Stave V as Scrooge expresses gratitude for securing his 'chance and hope of escaping' the fate of his dead partner. Compare this with Stave I (pages 3–5) where Scrooge refuses to believe in Marley's Ghost.

Key events

- Back in his own house, Scrooge is satisfied that his bedpost, bed, and room are all his own and he realises that the time before him is also 'his own, to make amends in!'
- He rushes to get dressed and reminds himself of the events that have taken place since the visit of Jacob Marley. Because he does not know what day it is, he opens the window to shout and find out from a passing boy.
- On learning that it is Christmas Day, Scrooge instructs the boy to go and buy the prize turkey from the poulterers and have it delivered to Bob Cratchit's house, offering a generous sum in exchange.
- Washed, shaved and dressed in his best clothes, he mingles in the streets with the Christmas crowds. Bumping into one of the portly gentlemen that visited him to ask for a donation, he offers him a very large sum of money to help the poor.
- He makes his way to his nephew, Fred's house, where he is made very welcome and joins in their party with Fred, his niece, Topper and the 'plump sister'.
- The next morning Scrooge makes sure he gets to the office before Bob Cratchit, who is unaccustomedly late.
- He puts on his fiercest voice and summons Bob to his office. Rather than firing him for being late, as Bob fears, he tells him that he will raise his salary and assist his family.
- He tells Bob to make up the fires and purchase a new coal scuttle.
- The narrator tells us that Scrooge was better than his word and did all he promised, becoming a second father to Tiny Tim, 'as good a master, and as good a man' as anyone knew.

REVISION TIP

When you explore plot, think about how some events act as a contrast to others and how certain events are echoed in other parts of the story.

Knowledge PLOT

6 Stave V

Key moments

Narrative/Character/Action	Significance	Key quotation
Scrooge is generous with the unknown boy who fetches the poulterer to deliver a turkey to Bob Cratchit.	Christmas is no longer a 'humbug' to Scrooge. Just as he promised the Phantom, he is 'honouring' Christmas 'in his heart'.	'"I am as light as a feather, I am as happy as an angel, I am as merry as a schoolboy. I am as giddy as a drunken man. A merry Christmas to everybody! A happy New Year to all the world!"'
Scrooge offers the portly gentleman a donation to his charity.	Scrooge is generous with his donation.	'"Not a farthing less. A great many back-payments are included in it, I assure you."'
Scrooge is reconciled with his nephew, Fred.	Scrooge has realised the value of family.	'"Will you let me in, Fred?" 'Let him in! It is a mercy he didn't shake his arm off. He was at home in five minutes. Nothing could be heartier.'
Scrooge gives Bob a raise with immediate effect and promises to help him with his family.	Scrooge has recognised his responsibility to his own employee, and those around him.	'"A merry Christmas, Bob!" said Scrooge, with an earnestness that could not be mistaken, as he clapped him on the back.' '"A merrier Christmas, Bob, my good fellow, than I have given you, for many a year! I'll raise your salary, and endeavour to assist your struggling family…"'
Scrooge has learned the lessons that the Spirits have taught him.	Scrooge continues to demonstrate the good qualities the experience has awakened in him.	'Scrooge was better than his word. He did it all, and infinitely more;'

Retrieval

6

Answer the questions below. Cover the answers column with a piece of paper and write down as many as you can. Check and repeat.

	Questions	Answers
1	What does Scrooge intend to do with the time that he now sees is 'his own'?	Use it to 'make amends in'
2	Complete the quotation: '"I am as light as a ______, I am as happy as an ______, I am as merry as a ______. I am as giddy as a ______ man."'	'"I am as light as a <u>feather</u>, I am as happy as an <u>angel</u>, I am as merry as a <u>schoolboy</u>. I am as giddy as a <u>drunken</u> man."'
3	What does Scrooge offer the 'portly gentleman'?	A sizeable donation to his charity, to make up for many years of giving nothing
4	Why does Scrooge want to get to the office before Bob Cratchit?	He wants to trick Bob into thinking he is in trouble before surprising him with the offer of a raise in salary
5	Complete the quotation: '"He sha'n't know who sends it. It's twice ______ ______ ______ ______ ______!"'	'"He sha'n't know who sends it. It's twice <u>the</u> <u>size</u> <u>of</u> <u>Tiny</u> <u>Tim</u>!"'

Put paper here

Previous questions

Now go back and use these questions to check your knowledge of previous topics.

	Questions	Answers
1	What nickname does one of the wealthy businessmen use when referring to Scrooge?	Old Scratch
2	Name two of the characters in the sordid shop where Scrooge's stolen possessions are being traded.	Two from: Old Joe / a laundress / a charwoman / an undertaker
3	Name three items that were stolen from the dead 'Scrooge' to sell in the sordid shop.	Three from: sleeve-buttons / sheets / towels / sugar-tongs / silver teaspoons / bed-curtains
4	How did the three thieves explain why it was so easy to steal from the dead man?	They say "He frightened every one away from him, when he was alive", so he died alone, with nobody to protect his property

Put paper here

7 Writer's methods

What are the writer's methods?

'Methods' refer to the ways a writer presents their ideas: anything they choose to do to show the story, characters, and ideas. This means the larger structural methods such as the big events of the text, their order, and how characters are used during the story. It also means the smaller aspects of text such as metaphor and language choices.

LINK

See page 2 for a note about the structure of the story.

REMEMBER

In the exam, you will be expected to write about Dickens' methods in telling the story. You will never be asked merely to retell the story.

Genre and narrative voice

Dickens brings together conventions from a range of different literary **genres**, or categories. *A Christmas Carol* is part ghost story, part parable, and part fairy tale.

Dickens' very distinctive **narrative voice** means that readers feel included in Scrooge's journey; we trust the writer as a reliable storyteller who takes us into his confidence.

This is achieved through a range of literary techniques but principally through a friendly, conversational voice and Dickens' use of **direct address**.

REVISION TIP

Dickens uses the traditional fairy-tale story introduction, 'Once upon a time', to alert readers to the improbable nature of Scrooge's story.

Examples of direct address

The story begins as if in the middle of a conversation with the reader: 'Marley was dead, to begin with.'

Dickens uses the **second person** form, 'you': 'You will therefore permit me to repeat, emphatically, that Marley was as dead as a door-nail'.
However, the majority of the novel is written from the point of view of a 'third person', **omniscient** narrator.

Sometimes Dickens writes as if we have interrupted him with a question, as he seems to 'answer us': 'Scrooge knew he was dead? Of course he did. How could it be otherwise?'

In places, we feel like we are sitting next to Dickens as he tells the story: 'The curtains of his bed were drawn aside, I tell you, by a hand […] and Scrooge […] found himself face to face with the unearthly visitor who drew them: as close to it as I am now to you […]'.

At the end of the story, the reader is reminded of the special writer/reader relationship throughout the story: '…it was always said of him, that he knew how to keep Christmas well, if any man alive possessed the knowledge. May that be truly said of us, and all of us! And so, as Tiny Tim observed, God bless Us, Every One!'

Tone

The **tone** is consistently informal and even 'jokey', with humour present throughout. We sometimes describe this as a 'self-conscious' style of writing, as the writer is drawing the reader's attention to his own choice of words, phrases, and figurative speech, in an engaging way. Some examples are:

Place in the story	Key quotation
Right at the start, the narrator includes some thoughts on the appropriateness, or otherwise, of the well-known simile 'as dead as a door-nail' that he has just used to describe Marley.	'Mind! I don't mean to say […] what there is particularly dead about a door-nail. I might have been inclined, myself, to regard a coffin-nail as the deadest piece of ironmongery in the trade.'
In Scrooge's quip to Marley's Ghost.	'"There's more of gravy than of grave about you, whatever you are!"'
Describing the young Cratchits' faces after their Christmas lunch.	'… steeped in sage and onion to the eyebrows!'
Whole sections that are comical in themselves, such as Topper's pursuit of the 'sister' at Fred's party.	'The way he went after that plump sister […] was an outrage on the credulity of human nature. Knocking down the fire-irons, tumbling over the chairs, bumping against the piano, smothering himself among the curtains, wherever she went, there went he!'

Vocabulary and descriptive writing

Dickens is known for his use of quite long sentences and precise word choices that express complex ideas.

Dickens further engages the reader using powerful descriptions of some characters. He uses an accumulation of adjectives to achieve a comical effect. Scrooge is initially described like this:

'Oh! ❶ But he was a tight-fisted hand at the grindstone, Scrooge! ❶ a squeezing, wrenching, grasping, scraping, clutching, ❷ covetous, old sinner!' ❸

❶ This 'sketch' of Scrooge begins and ends with an exclamation mark – and includes another after his name, in the middle of the sentence, to emphasise his negative qualities.

❷ Dickens uses five present participles – 'squeezing, wrenching, grasping, scraping, clutching' – to make the picture more immediate, as if Scrooge stands before us 'doing' all those things.

❸ At the end of this list of negative qualities, Dickens calls Scrooge an 'old sinner' which gives a comic twist to the portrait of a thoroughly unpleasant sounding man.

Dickens uses a slightly different approach when it comes to describing the appearance of characters – as opposed to their 'natures'. In some descriptive passages, Dickens goes into great detail; for example, when describing the appearance of the Ghost of Christmas Present, where he describes the Ghost's physical qualities as well as his clothes and accessories. In other instances, Dickens offers only a brief description; for example, when he introduces Mrs Cratchit.

Knowledge METHODS

7 Writer's methods

Dialogue

Dialogue creates 'drama' within the novel, as each of Dickens' characters has a distinctive 'voice' – apart from the Ghost of Christmas Yet to Come. It has no voice at all, signalling to Scrooge through hand gestures alone.

<table>
<tr><th>Character and voice</th><th>What it reveals</th><th>Key quotation</th></tr>
<tr><td>Scrooge's short 'barking' style of some phrases.</td><td>His negative qualities.</td><td>'"Humbug!"'</td></tr>
<tr><td>Fezziwig's genuinely jolly way of speaking.</td><td>His encouraging nature; explains why he was such an inspiration to the young apprentices in Scrooge's youth.</td><td>• '"Yo ho, there! Ebenezer! Dick!"'
• '"Yo ho, my boys!"'
• '"Clear away, my lads, and let's have lots of room here! Hilli-ho, Dick! Chirrup, Ebenezer!"'</td></tr>
<tr><td>The Ghosts of Christmas Past and Christmas Present each have slightly different 'spectral' voices.
• 'Past' is more detached; it tends to make observations rather than engaging in conversation.
• 'Present', the more genial ghost, fully engages with Scrooge, answering questions and appearing more responsive.</td><td>• 'Past' wants Scrooge's memories to remind him of the qualities he had before, and to reflect upon them.
• 'Present' is more concerned with developing Scrooge's social conscience, so that he will act upon lessons learned.</td><td>• Past: '"Remember it!" cried Scrooge with fervour; "I could walk it blindfold."
"Strange to have forgotten it for so many years!" observed the Ghost. "Let us go on."'
• Present: '"Spirit," said Scrooge, with an interest he had never felt before, "tell me if Tiny Tim will live.""I see a vacant seat," replied the Ghost, "in the poor chimney-corner, and a crutch without an owner, carefully preserved. If these shadows remain unaltered by the Future, the child will die."'</td></tr>
<tr><td>Ghost of Christmas Yet to Come has no voice at all, signalling to Scrooge through hand gestures, leaving Scrooge to interpret the sights and sounds of the 'future'.</td><td>'Yet to Come' intends to stimulate Scrooge's imagination about what the future might hold for him, which is achieved more effectively in silence.</td><td>• 'The Spirit answered not, but pointed onward with its hand.'
• 'The Phantom spread its dark robe before him for a moment, like a wing; and withdrawing it, revealed a room by daylight, where a mother and her children were.'</td></tr>
<tr><td>The Ghost of Jacob Marley speaks mainly using negatives.</td><td>Reflects his truly miserable existence as a wandering spirit.</td><td>• '"I cannot rest, I cannot stay, I cannot linger anywhere. My spirit never walked beyond our counting-house – mark me! – in life my spirit never roved beyond…"'
• '"No rest, no peace. Incessant torture of remorse."'</td></tr>
</table>

Character and voice	What it reveals	Key quotation
The 'portly gentlemen' who call on Scrooge looking for a charitable donation speak formally and grammatically correctly.	Dickens makes sure to distinguish between the classes through the way the more and the less privileged characters speak.	'"At this festive season of the year, Mr. Scrooge," said the gentleman, taking up a pen, "it is more than usually desirable that we should make some slight provision for the Poor and destitute, who suffer greatly at the present time."'
Bob and the rest of the Cratchit family speak more informally.	This illustrates the gap between the rich and the poor.	'"Why, bless your heart alive, my dear, how late you are!" said Mrs. Cratchit [...] '"We'd a deal of work to finish up last night," replied the girl [...] '"Well! Never mind so long as you are come," said Mrs. Cratchit. "Sit ye down before the fire, my dear, and have a warm, Lord bless ye!"'
The lower-class characters in Old Joe's sordid shop speak in an approximation of an East London accent.	Only the characters from the wealthy and educated classes speak in '**standard English**'.	'"If he wanted to keep 'em after he was dead, a wicked old screw", pursued the woman, "why wasn't he natural in his lifetime? If he had been, he'd have had somebody to look after him when he was struck with Death, instead of lying gasping out his last there, alone by himself."'

LINK

See Characters pages 28-57 for more on how Dickens creates distinctive characters through how they speak.

Irony

Another feature of Dickens' writing is the use of **irony**:

- Dickens uses irony to highlight Scrooge's cynicism and his disapproval of Fred. When Fred makes his speech to Scrooge about Christmas time being 'a good time' – a speech that extends over 14 lines – Scrooge makes the ironic comment:

> '"You're quite a powerful speaker, sir [...] I wonder you don't go into Parliament."'

- He also uses it to highlight how appreciative the Cratchits are of what they have, however little it may seem to an outsider; for example when Mrs Cratchit brings her Christmas pudding to the table we learn that it was a very small pudding by the way Dickens writes that nobody called it 'small':

> 'Everybody had something to say about it, but nobody said or thought it was at all a small pudding for a large family. It would have been flat **heresy** to do so. Any Cratchit would have blushed to hint at such a thing.'

Knowledge METHODS

7 Writer's methods

Figurative language

Dickens also uses **figurative language** (**similes**, **metaphors**, **symbolism**, and **personification**) to enliven the writing and to draw special attention to the ideas being presented.

Figurative language

Similes

- Old Marley: 'as dead as a door-nail'
- The Phantom: 'coming, like a mist along the ground, towards him'
- Scrooge: '"... as light as a feather, I am as happy as an angel, I am as merry as a schoolboy"'

Metaphors

- Scrooge says of Christmas: '"A poor excuse for picking a man's pocket every twenty-fifth of December!"'
- Little Fan's nature: 'brimful of glee'

Personification

Scrooge's house looking out of place next to other houses in the street: 'one could scarcely help fancying it must have run there when it was a young house, playing at hide-and-seek with other houses, and forgotten the way out again.'

Symbolism

The 'wretched' children concealed in the skirts of the Ghost of Christmas Present: '"This boy is Ignorance. This girl is Want."'

REVISION TIP

In using the children as symbols for Ignorance and Want, Dickens gives a human face to abstract ideas to make the reader think about the ideas afresh.

Key terms **Make sure you can write a definition for these key terms.**

direct address   figurative language   genre   heresy
metaphor   narrative voice   omniscient
personification   second person   simile
standard English   symbolism   tone

Retrieval

Answer the questions below. Cover the answers column with a piece of paper and write down as many as you can. Check and repeat.

	Questions	Answers
1	*A Christmas Carol* is a mixture of literary genres; name two of them.	Two from: ghost story / parable / fairy tale
2	How does Dickens make the reader feel that they can trust the narrative voice in *A Christmas Carol*?	By using a friendly, conversational voice and direct address
3	Which types of characters use what is typically seen as standard English in *A Christmas Carol?*	The wealthy and the educated classes
4	Give an example of the use of irony when Scrooge is talking to Fred.	'"You're quite a powerful speaker, sir [...] I wonder you don't go into Parliament."' (when Scrooge suggests that Fred should go into Parliament)
5	Name the figure of speech used in this example: He was feeling 'as light as a feather'.	Simile
6	Name the figure of speech used in this example: a '"poor excuse for picking a man's pocket every twenty-fifth of December"'.	Metaphor
7	Which of the following is a metaphor: 'dead as a door-nail' or 'brimful of glee'?	'brimful of glee'
8	Complete the quotation: '"This _____ is Ignorance. This girl is _____."'	'"This <u>boy</u> is Ignorance. This girl is <u>Want</u>."'
9	What figure of speech is used in the quotation in question 9?	Symbolism

Put paper here

Previous questions

Now go back and use these questions to check your knowledge of previous topics.

	Questions	Answers
1	What does Scrooge intend to do with the time that he now sees is 'his own'?	Use it to 'make amends in'
2	What does Scrooge offer the 'portly gentleman'?	A sizeable donation to his charity, to make up for many years of giving nothing

Put paper here

Now turn to page 115 and complete Practice question 12.

Knowledge CHARACTERS

8 Ebenezer Scrooge

Characters Scrooge interacts with directly

Scrooge is present throughout the story, while other characters come and go.

In the 'present' time, Scrooge has interactions with eight sets of characters.

Characters Scrooge interacts with directly

- Fred – Scrooge's nephew
- Bob Cratchit – Scrooge's clerk
- The Ghost of Jacob Marley
- The Ghost of Christmas Past
- The Ghost of Christmas Present
- The Ghost of Christmas Yet to Come
- Two 'portly gentlemen'
- Unnamed boy

LINK

Find out more about Bob, Fred, Marley, and the Ghosts on pages 34–52.

REVISION TIP

Take note of how character traits and attitudes are established in the early part of the story, and then how some are developed or even reversed as the narrative progresses. Track these character developments as you revise the plot.

Characters Scrooge visits with the Spirits

In the various scenes that Scrooge is taken to, he sees many characters but has no interactions with any of them.

Characters Scrooge visits with the Spirits

The Ghost of Christmas Past

- Scrooge as a boy
- Little Fan
- Schoolmaster
- Old Fezziwig and family
- Dick Wilkins
- Belle and her family

The Ghost of Christmas Present

- Bob Cratchit, Mrs Cratchit, Tiny Tim, Peter, Martha, Belinda Cratchit, two young Cratchits
- Miners, lighthouse keepers, sailors
- Fred and his wife, Scrooge's niece, Topper, Scrooge's niece's two sisters
- Two 'wretched children': Ignorance and Want

The Ghost of Christmas Yet to Come

- Business associates of Scrooge
- Old Joe; a laundress; a charwoman; an undertaker's man
- Caroline and her husband
- Cratchit family (minus Tiny Tim)

LINK

Find out more about some of these characters on pages 49–52.

The presentation of Scrooge

Method of presentation	What this reveals about Scrooge
Physical appearance/ qualities	Scrooge is described with: 'pointed nose, shrivelled [...] cheek, stiffened [...] gait; [...] eyes red, [...] thin lips blue; [...] grating voice [...] wiry chin' (in Stave I).
What he does in the story	Scrooge develops from a 'tight-fisted [...] old sinner' to 'as good a friend [...] master [...] man' as any in the world, through Marley's warning and the intervention of the Spirits. His 'reclamation' (**redemption**) is the focus of the whole story.
What he says in the story	Scrooge starts off by saying Christmas is a '"Humbug!"' His attitude towards the poor and destitute is shocking, as his idea of charity is to send them to prison or to the workhouse. He says: '"If they would rather die [...] they had better do it, and decrease the surplus population."' However, Scrooge ends the story quite differently, saying: '"A merrier Christmas, Bob, my good fellow, than I have given you for many a year! I'll raise your salary, and endeavour to assist your struggling family."'
Observations of other characters	Most other characters don't have good things to say about Scrooge: • From Mrs Cratchit: '"an odious, stingy, hard, unfeeling man"' • From the charwoman: '"a wicked old screw"' • From Fred: '"He's a comical old fellow [...] that's the truth: and not so pleasant as he might be."'
Comparison/ contrast with other characters	Scrooge is **contrasted** with his nephew, Fred, in Stave I: • Of Scrooge: 'cold', 'no wind [...] bitterer', 'no wintry weather' could 'chill him' • Of Fred: 'He had so heated himself with rapid walking [...] that he was all in a glow; his face was ruddy and handsome; his eyes sparkled'. And with his old employer, Fezziwig, in Stave II: • Scrooge to his clerk: '"But I suppose you must have the whole day. Be here all the earlier next morning."' The clerk promised that he would; and Scrooge walked out with a growl. • Fezziwig to his apprentices: '"Yo ho, my boys! [...] No more work to-night. Christmas Eve, Dick. Christmas, Ebenezer! [...] Clear away, my lads, and let's have lots of room here! Hilli-ho, Dick! Chirrup, Ebenezer!"'

8 Ebenezer Scrooge

Method of presentation	What this reveals about Scrooge
How he expresses himself	• Scrooge often speaks in abrupt and harsh sentences in the early part of the novel: '"Bah!"', '"Humbug!"', '"I wish to be left alone."', '"Are there no prisons?"' • Occasionally we see his humorous nature, even in his bitter words: '"…every idiot who goes about with 'Merry Christmas' on his lips, should be boiled with his own pudding, and buried with a stake of holly through his heart. He should!"' • As his journey of 'reclamation' progresses, we see a 'softer' side of Scrooge emerging through what he says and how he says it: Stave II: 'Then […] he said, in pity for his former self, "Poor boy!" and cried again.' Stave III: '"Spirit," said Scrooge, with an interest he had never felt before, "tell me if Tiny Tim will live."' Stave IV: '"If there is any person […] who feels emotion caused by this man's death," said Scrooge quite agonised, "show that person to me, Spirit, I beseech you!"'

REVISION TIP

Make sure you focus on revising the development of Scrooge's character through the story – don't just think about him as the mean old man from Stave I.

REVISION TIP

The manner in which characters act and react towards each other gives a good guide to their feelings and attitudes. Look for parts of the story where these attitudes change or develop.

Function

- Symbolises greed and selfishness – at the beginning of the story, Scrooge is consumed by his own greed and selfishness.
- Represents the theme of social inequality – Scrooge's character development allows Dickens to present the divide between the wealthy and the poor.
- Reveals the importance of family – Scrooge's experience teaches him that his greed and refusal to care for others denies him the joy of family and friends.
- Shows transformation and redemption – Scrooge's transformation from a miser to a person determined to do good in the world shows that change is possible.
- Demonstrates the value of charity and helping others – Scrooge's change could inspire readers to change themselves and try to embody the Christmas spirit which Dickens portrays.

Key terms **Make sure you can write a definition for these key terms**

contrast *function* *redemption*

Writing about Ebenezer Scrooge

Sample answer 1: not a strong answer

Here is an extract from a student response to this question, with the examiner's annotations and final comments. It receives less than half marks.

Extract from Stave I, from: 'This lunatic, in letting Scrooge's nephew out, had let two other people in…' to: 'Scrooge resumed his labours with an improved opinion of himself, and in a more facetious temper than was usual with him.'

REVISION TIP

Compare the use of Dickens' text in each sample answer. What matters is how quotations are used: in sample answer 2 text is not only quoted but commented upon.

> Starting with this extract, how does Dickens present Scrooge's attitude towards others?
>
> **[30 marks]**

Scrooge has a bad attitude towards others in this extract. ❶ He is already in a bad mood with Fred, and then the portly gentlemen ask Scrooge for money. ❷ Scrooge is not very polite when they ask whether he is Scrooge or Marley, just telling them that Marley is dead and not showing a kind attitude to his dead partner or to the gentlemen. ❸ Little do the gentlemen know that Scrooge will not give them anything as he is so 'tight-fisted'. ❹ When the gentlemen talk about giving the poor 'meat and drink' and 'warmth', Scrooge has no pity ❺ and suggests that they should go to prisons or workhouses as they are still open, and he describes them as 'useful'. ❻ His attitude is so bad that he thinks if the poor had 'rather die' than go to the workhouse they should get on with it! ❼

❶ Addresses the question directly, although in a simplistic way, terming Scrooge's attitude as 'bad'

❷ Offers some basic context for the events in the extract

❸ Maintains a straightforward focus on attitude and makes a reasonable point about Scrooge's apparent lack of concern for Marley

❹ Makes an observation that reveals some understanding of Scrooge's character and includes a quotation about Scrooge, taken from the narrator's earlier description of him

❺ A little relevant use of text to support a point about Scrooge's attitude of no pity for those people who lack 'meat and drink' and 'warmth'

❻ Quotation of 'useful' reveals some understanding of attitude but would be improved by further explanation

❼ Keeps the focus and shows some understanding of Scrooge

Examiner's comments

This response shows some focus, as it begins with a reference to Scrooge's attitude. The reference to 'bad mood', although a little generalised, is an apt description of Scrooge's attitude to others.

Some relevant references to text are included and there is some explanation, which would benefit from more supporting textual references. There is little sense of the writer's methods.

8 Ebenezer Scrooge

Sample answer 2: a strong answer

Here is an extract from a student response to the question on page 31, with the examiner's annotations and final comments. It receives high marks.

Dickens uses the narrative voice and Scrooge's own words and actions to reveal Scrooge's attitude towards others as careless and dismissive. ❶ The portly gentlemen courteously remove their hats and bow, but Scrooge's manner is blunt in announcing Marley's death: 'Mr. Marley has been dead these seven years.' ❷ The narrator describes Scrooge's frown at the word 'liberality', adopting Scrooge's own perspective on the word by using the qualifier 'ominous'. ❸ The gentlemen's appeal is sidestepped by Scrooge, showing his indifference to the sufferings of others by asking almost teasing, questions about prisons. ❹ He cites 'prisons', 'Union workhouses', the 'Treadmill' and, finally, the 'Poor Law' in a facetious manner. ❺ He adopts a tone of 'mock' civility to express his 'gladness' that various corrective institutions are still in operation. 'Oh! I was afraid [...] that something had occurred to stop them in their useful course.' ❻ The narrator contrasts the ways that the characters converse to emphasise Scrooge's attitude to others. The gentlemen's speech is polite and mainly 'said', while Scrooge's lines are reported as being delivered in a more challenging form: 'asked', 'demanded' or 'returned', highlighting his combative attitude. ❼ In addition to the gestures of refusal, 'Scrooge frowned, and shook his head', Scrooge also uses negative phrases: 'Nothing', 'I don't make merry', 'I can't afford', 'It's not my business' to match his attitude towards others, ❽ and he refers to the poor and the destitute, contemptuously, as 'idle'. ❾

❶ Clear focus on the question; three methods of presentation are identified and exemplified in the answer

❷ Both actions and speech are considered and text is used to support ideas

❸ This is a perceptive point about the narrator switching to Scrooge's perspective

❹ Insightful comment on Scrooge's teasing

❺ Short quotations used well and also picking up on Scrooge's 'facetious' temper mentioned at the end of the extract

❻ Good point about Scrooge's 'tone'

❼ Useful analysis of contrasting modes of speech

❽ Useful analysis of Scrooge's negative gestures and phrases

❾ Returns to the focus of the question in a concise way

Examiner's comments

This is thoughtful and detailed work which is well-focused on the demands of the question. The approach is critical and supported with a judicious selection of examples. Explanations are well-supported from the text, and there is a sense of exploration of both meaning and method.

Retrieval

Answer the questions below. Cover the answers column with a piece of paper and write down as many as you can. Check and repeat.

Questions	Answers
1 Name three characters that Scrooge sees when he is with the Ghost of Christmas Past.	Three from: Scrooge as a boy / Little Fan / the Schoolmaster / Fezziwig / Dick Wilkins / Belle and family
2 Which four characters appear when Scrooge is with the Ghost of Christmas Yet to Come?	Old Joe; Bob Cratchit; Caroline; the laundress
3 Name three of Scrooge's physical features, as described by Dickens.	Three from: 'pointed nose' / 'shrivelled [...] cheek' / 'stiffened [...] gait' / 'eyes red' / 'thin lips blue' / 'grating voice' / 'wiry chin'
4 What makes Scrooge develop from a 'tight-fisted [...] old sinner' to 'as good a friend [...] master [...] man' as any in the world?	The Ghost of Marley's warning and the intervention of the Spirits
5 Complete the quotation: '"I'll raise your ______, and endeavour to assist your __________ family"'	'"I'll raise your <u>salary</u>, and endeavour to assist your <u>struggling</u> family"'
6 Which character describes Scrooge as '"an odious, stingy, hard, unfeeling man"'?	Mrs Cratchit
7 Name two characters that Dickens uses as contrasts to Scrooge.	Fred; Fezziwig
8 Complete the quotation: '"every idiot who goes about with 'Merry Christmas' on his lips, should be ______ with his own ________"'.	'"every idiot who goes about with 'Merry Christmas' on his lips, should be <u>boiled</u> with his own <u>pudding</u>"'.
9 Complete the quotation: '"Spirit," said Scrooge, with an interest he had never felt before, "tell me if ____ ____ ____ ____."'	'"Spirit," said Scrooge, with an interest he had never felt before, "tell me if <u>Tiny</u> <u>Tim</u> <u>will</u> <u>live</u>."'
10 Name one of Scrooge's functions, in addition to his role as a focus for the whole story.	One from: symbolises greed and selfishness / represents the theme of social inequality / reveals the importance of family / shows transformation and redemption / demonstrates the value of charity and helping others

(Put paper here)

Previous questions

Now go back and use these questions to check your knowledge of previous topics.

Questions	Answers
1 How does Dickens make the reader feel that they can trust the narrative voice in *A Christmas Carol*?	By using a friendly conversational voice and direct address
2 Name the figure of speech used in this example: He was feeling as 'light as a feather'.	Simile

(Put paper here)

Now turn to page 113 and complete Practice question 10.

9 Bob Cratchit

The presentation of Bob Cratchit

Bob Cratchit appears in Staves I and V, and in visions in Staves III and IV. He is not actually named until Stave III – up to this point he is referred to as Scrooge's clerk.

Method of presentation	What this reveals about Bob Cratchit
Bob's physical appearance/ qualities	• The only physical description of him is 'little' Bob, who has 'no great-coat', but wears a 'white comforter' (scarf) and 'threadbare clothes'. • The description of Bob going 'down a slide […] twenty times, in honour of its being Christmas Eve' and then running home to play 'blindman's-buff' suggests a childlike ability to have fun. • Bob is presented as a loving family man, thankful for his wife and six children, including Tiny Tim. 'Bob held his withered little hand in his, as if he loved the child, and wished to keep him by his side'.
What Bob does	• Bob works hard in poor working conditions, confined to 'a dismal little cell' on Scrooge's premises, 'a sort of tank', which suggests he is constantly being watched by Scrooge. • Bob exchanges Christmas greetings with Fred, 'cordially', and infuriates Scrooge when he 'involuntarily applauded' after Fred's speech about Christmas. • After Christmas dinner, Bob proposes a toast to Scrooge, calling him 'the Founder of the Feast' and, when Mrs Cratchit protests, he mildly insists, '"My dear," said Bob, "the children! Christmas Day."' • In Stave IV, Bob shows great strength of character following the 'death' of Tiny Tim. He encourages the family never to forget Tim.
What Bob says	• Bob says little at work, but is respected in his own home. Whenever he speaks, he shows a kind and encouraging nature: ○ he says Tiny Tim is: '"As good as gold […] and better"' ○ he praises Mrs Cratchit's cooking: '"Oh a wonderful pudding!"' ○ 'he praised the industry and speed of Mrs. Cratchit and the girls' in sewing Tiny Tim's shroud.

Method of presentation	What this reveals about Bob Cratchit
What others think or say about Bob	• Scrooge thinks Bob is a 'lunatic' to talk about '"a merry Christmas"' on only '"fifteen shillings a-week"'. After his experience with the Spirits, Scrooge revises his opinion and becomes a good friend to Bob and his family. • Like all of his children, Martha adores Bob and 'didn't like to see him disappointed' when he thinks she isn't coming home for Christmas. • Fred is always courteous to Bob, showing him compassion after Tiny Tim's 'death'.
How Bob compares/ contrasts with other characters	• It is possible to compare Bob (who has a loving relationship with his children and is determined to enjoy Christmas with them all) with Scrooge's father (who would not allow the boy Scrooge home for the Christmas holidays).
How Bob expresses himself	• Bob is polite and deferential when he answers Scrooge. • When he talks to his family, his tone is always affectionate, and he calls his wife and children '"my dear(s)"' or '"my boy"'. • He expresses his gratitude for any kindness shown, such as when he describes Fred's condolences over Tiny Tim's death: '"Now, it wasn't," cried Bob, "for the sake of anything he might be able to do for us, so much as for his kind way, that this was quite delightful."'

REVISION TIP

Pick four moments from the story which you think are important for understanding the character of Bob Cratchit and explain what you learn from each.

Function

- Represents the working poor – Bob is an overworked and underpaid clerk, and Dickens uses his plight to represent the poor working conditions and low pay of many working-class people in the Victorian era.
- Defies Scrooge's ideas of poverty – Bob is poor, but he is kind, generous, and hard-working. He challenges ideas about the poor being lazy and undeserving, views held by Scrooge at the start of the story.
- Provides a foil to Scrooge – Bob is the opposite of Scrooge, representing kindness and generosity contrasted with Scrooge's cruelty and greed.
- Helps Scrooge to change – Bob's kindness and generosity help Scrooge to eventually change his ways.
- Demonstrates the idea of Christmas spirit – Bob exemplifies Dickens' values of Christmas spirit, such as forgiveness and compassion. He toasts to Scrooge's health despite Scrooge's terrible treatment of him, and is open to accepting Scrooge's remorse.
- Represents the value of family – Bob is determined to hold his family together, and his family shows great love and joy despite their poverty.

9 Bob Cratchit

Writing about Bob Cratchit

Sample answer 1: not a strong answer

Here is an extract from a student response to this question, with the examiner's annotations and final comments. It receives less than half marks.

Extract from Stave IV, from: '"… And there is your father at the door!"' to: "It really seemed as if he had known our Tiny Tim, and felt with us."'

> Starting with this extract, how does Dickens present Bob Cratchit as a sympathetic character?
>
> **[30 marks]**

This passage begins with Bob Cratchit arriving home. All of his family members are pleased to see him. Nobody wants Bob to grieve over Tiny Tim's death, they want him to be cheerful as usual. **1** *All of Bob's children try to cheer him up by helping him get his tea; this proves that Bob is a loveable, kind father.* **2** *The little Cratchits don't understand what has happened to Tiny Tim, they just want a cuddle from their dad.* **3** *When Bob visits Tiny Tim, he gets a grip of himself and maybe tells himself that it's for the best, and that Tim is no longer suffering. He tells himself this so that he can kiss his son's face and get on with his life.* **4** *Readers feel sorry to see a grown man crying, so this is a good change in Bob.* **5** *Bob is also shown to be a bit slow in the head when he doesn't understand how Fred knew that Mrs Cratchit is a good woman because he doesn't get that this is just a polite way of saying 'your wife'.* **6** *This also makes Bob quite a sympathetic character because he is a bit simple.* **7**

1 This is factually correct but under-developed and lacking in an immediate focus on the question.

2 There is a limited attempt to use evidence from the narrative to support a positive presentation of Bob.

3 This statement is not fully convincing, although the implication that the youngsters don't fully 'understand' death is a fair one.

4 There is a lot of guesswork here in relation to Tiny Tim's 'suffering' and the even less convincing idea that Bob wishes to 'get on with his life'.

5 This is an awkwardly phrased attempt at the concept of reader sympathy, but the lack of textual support creates some ambiguity here.

6 This is a possible personal interpretation.

7 This is the first direct mention of a 'sympathetic response' to Bob, but Dickens' methods have not yet been explored.

Examiner's comments

This is a largely narrative approach with some awareness of implicit meaning but limited attempts to consider Dickens' methods. The student draws a few inferences about Bob's sympathetic qualities without consistently making these explicit.

Sample answer 2: a strong answer

Here is an extract from a student response, to this question with the examiner's annotations and final comments. It receives high marks.

Dickens uses a variety of methods to present Bob Cratchit sympathetically. The narrative voice reveals sympathy for Bob, his family reacts sympathetically towards him, and Bob's own actions and words attract reader sympathy. ❶

Mrs Cratchit and the family have been waiting for Bob's return, and Mrs Cratchit 'hurried out to meet him', emphasising her concern for her husband, and also inviting the reader's concern. The narrator does not merely describe Bob 'in his comforter' but, in an aside, indicated by dashes, he confides '—he had need of it, poor fellow—', channelling the reader's sympathy towards him. ❷ The children are shown to compete to help Bob to his tea, and comfort him, in their own innocent way, by each laying their 'little cheek' against his, revealing Dickens' use of actions and emotive vocabulary, drawing the reader's sympathy towards Bob. ❸

Bob's cheerfulness, despite his distress, attracts admiration as he speaks 'pleasantly' to his family, and speaking of his 'little, little child', Bob 'broke down all at once'. The narrator tells the reader directly that Bob 'couldn't help it' since, 'If he could have helped it, he and his child would have been farther apart perhaps than they were.' This is a poignant reminder of Bob's sympathetic quality of devotion to his son. ❹

Continued

❶ Clear sense of purpose from the outset

❷ Clear, supported explanation of the narrator's intervention

❸ This is a sensitive and clearly explained response to the writer's methods.

❹ This distinguishes perceptively between the narrative voice 'narrating events' and the moments when the narrative voice 'comments' on those events. The effect of this is linked purposefully to the question.

9 Bob Cratchit

The tender picture of Bob's private moments with Tiny Tim is sensitively drawn. The narrator calls the grieving father 'poor Bob' and, by reminding the reader of Tiny Tim's youth and frailty when Bob kisses his 'little face', increases our sympathy for Bob. ❺ *Initially I was puzzled by the narrator's description of Bob, as 'quite happy' here; but on reflection, I understand what Dickens achieves, increasing our admiration and sympathy for Bob, who must be reconciled to Tim's passing, to lead his family through their grief.* ❻

❺ The student offers further evidence of sensitivity to the writer's methods.

❻ This is evidence of personal engagement with the writing, both responding to the writing and reflecting upon Dickens' purpose in what he writes.

Examiner's comments

This is a detailed and insightful consideration of how the writer achieves a sympathetic response to Bob. Language receives careful and perceptive attention, and there is sensitivity both to the situation presented in the passage and to Dickens' methodology. Text is used purposefully to support the explanation.

REVISION TIP

Make a plan for how you would respond to this question, including which textual references you might include.

Retrieval

Answer the questions below. Cover the answers column with a piece of paper and write down as many as you can. Check and repeat.

	Questions	Answers
1	Dickens does not describe what Bob looks like in any detail. What single physical trait does Dickens mention?	Bob is sometimes called 'little Bob'
2	Which one of the following items of clothing does Bob wear to keep him warm: a greatcoat, a waistcoat, a white comforter, a woolly hat?	A white comforter
3	Complete the quotation: 'Bob held his ________ ____ hand in his, as if he loved the child, and wished to keep him by his ____'.	Bob held his withered little hand in his, as if he loved the child, and wished to keep him by his side'
4	Which two childlike activities does Dickens say that Bob takes part in?	Going down a slide, twenty times; rushing home to play 'blindman's-buff'
5	Complete the quotation: 'The clerk in the ____ involuntarily _________.'	'The clerk in the tank involuntarily applauded.'
6	When Mrs Cratchit objects to Bob's toast to Scrooge as the 'Founder of the Feast', how does Bob calm her down?	By reminding her of the presence of the children and that it is Christmas time
7	How much does Bob earn as clerk to Scrooge?	Fifteen shillings per week
8	Why does Scrooge think of Bob as 'lunatic'?	For talking about 'a merry Christmas' when he earns only 15 shillings per week
9	Which of Bob's children didn't want to see him disappointed?	Martha
10	To which character does Bob function as a foil?	Scrooge

Put paper here

Previous questions

Now go back and use these questions to check your knowledge of previous topics.

	Questions	Answers
1	Name three of Scrooge's physical features as described by Dickens.	Three from: 'pointed nose' / 'shrivelled [...] cheek' / 'stiffened [...] gait' / 'eyes red' / 'thin lips blue' / 'grating voice' / 'wiry chin'
2	What makes Scrooge develop from a 'tight-fisted [...] old sinner' to 'as good a friend [...] master [...] man' as any in the world?	The Ghost of Marley's warning and the intervention of the Spirits

Put paper here

Now turn to page 108 and complete Practice question 6.

10 Fred

The presentation of Fred

Fred – Scrooge's nephew – appears in Staves I and V, and in a vision in Stave III. He is not actually named until Stave III – up to this point he is referred to as Scrooge's nephew.

Method of presentation	What this reveals about Fred
Fred's physical appearance/qualities	• Fred is warm and glowing; 'his face was ruddy and handsome', and he has 'a cheerful voice'; he is always in a cheerful mood. • In Stave III Fred's laugh is described: 'Scrooge's nephew laughed […] holding his sides, rolling his head, and twisting his face.'
What Fred does	• He invites Scrooge for Christmas dinner and makes a speech defending Christmas as a good time, '"a kind, forgiving, charitable, pleasant time ..."' • He hosts a Christmas party first, as shown to Scrooge by the Ghost of Christmas Present, and then as the 'real' Fred in Stave V, where Scrooge enjoys a warm welcome.
What Fred says	• Fred says Christmas is the one time '"when men and women seem […] to open their shut-up hearts freely, and to think of people below them as if they really were fellow-passengers to the grave"'. • He is kind about his uncle: '"He's a comical old fellow […] and I have nothing to say against him."' Fred intends to give Scrooge '"the same chance every year, whether he likes it or not, for I pity him.'" • Fred has kind words about the loss of Tiny Tim: '"I am heartily sorry for it, Mr. Cratchit," he said, "and heartily sorry for your good wife."'
What others think or say about Fred	• Scrooge starts off thinking (and calling) Fred an '"idiot who goes about with 'Merry Christmas' on his lips"' – but changes his mind by the end. • Bob Cratchit reacts positively to Fred's speech about Christmas and expresses gratitude for Fred's response to Tiny Tim's 'death', noting his 'extraordinary kindness'.
How Fred compares/ contrasts with other characters	• Fred is directly compared with Scrooge in Stave I, where Scrooge's 'low temperature […] iced his office', but Fred's warmth makes him 'glow'. • They are in direct opposition on the subject of Christmas and despite Scrooge's downright rudeness, Fred leaves him amiably having tried very hard to 'be friends' with Scrooge.
How Fred speaks	• Fred speaks in a positive and cheery tone, reflecting his optimistic and genial personality: '"A merry Christmas, uncle! God save you!" cried a cheerful voice.' '"I want nothing from you; I ask nothing of you; why cannot we be friends?"' • To Bob Cratchit, he offers his condolences: '"If I can be of service to you in any way," he said, giving me his card, "that's where I live. Pray come to me."'

Function

- Serves as a foil to Scrooge – Fred represents what Scrooge could be like if he made different choices. Fred is kind, generous, and happy, while Scrooge is cruel, greedy and unhappy.
- Embodies Christmas spirit – Dickens presents the joy and love of Christmas through Fred's celebrations and willingness to welcome Scrooge to celebrate with his family.
- Represents the middle class – Fred is not as wealthy as Scrooge, so Dickens uses Fred to show the middle class.
- Provides Scrooge's connection to family – Fred is Scrooge's nephew, and he invites Scrooge to his Christmas parties every year. Fred's mother was Scrooge's sister, and Scrooge's refusal to accept Fred's invitations highlights his isolation.
- Acts as a role model for Scrooge – Through Fred, Dickens shows that money and happiness are not as closely intertwined as Scrooge believes at the start of the story.
- Provides an example of social responsibility – Fred treats Bob Cratchit better than Scrooge does, showing Dickens' views on how an employer should behave.

REVISION TIP

Exam questions never ask you just to write about a character. They link a character to a key idea and either ask how it is presented or ask you to make a judgement upon it. When revising, always think about how characters' actions can be linked to ideas.

10 Fred

Writing about Fred

Sample answer 1: not a strong answer

Here is an extract from a student response to this question, with the examiner's annotations and final comments. It receives less than half marks.

Extract from Stave I, from: '"A merry Christmas, uncle! God save you!" cried a cheerful voice.' to: '"[…] I believe that it *has* done me good, and *will* do me good; and I say, God bless it!"'

> Starting with this extract, how does Dickens present cheerful characters and their effect on Scrooge in *A Christmas Carol*? **[30 marks]**

Fred bursts into Scrooge's miserable office and immediately brightens the mood. ❶ He is described as being 'heated' whereas Scrooge is 'icy', which is a useful contrast. ❷ Fred tries to joke with his uncle, but Scrooge is not in the mood. Scrooge insults Fred by calling him 'poor' but Fred just laughs. ❸ He is disappointed that Scrooge refuses his invitation to dinner and makes a speech about everything that is wonderful about Christmas, ending with an emphatic, 'God bless it!'. ❹ Fred mentions the 'sacred name and origin' of Christmas, which shows that he appreciates its religious significance; he doesn't just love Christmas for the parties, although he knows how to throw a good Christmas party. ❺ It is important when Fred refers to life as a 'journey to the grave' because this is one of the most important themes in the book, especially for Scrooge. ❻ Another good thing about Fred is his kindness to Bob, who he knows must put up with his uncle's bad temper, and he speaks kindly to him on his way out. ❼

❶ Use of the word 'bursts' conveys Fred's exuberance. Reference to brightening the 'mood' is apt; 'cheerful' is implied but not stated.

❷ The physical description of Fred is not linked clearly to 'cheerful character'; the comparison to Scrooge is not irrelevant, but its relevance to 'cheerfulness' is not made explicit.

❸ Fred does more than 'just laugh' at Scrooge's comment; his lively response – not alluded to – would have been helpful in supporting the idea of Fred's cheerful character.

❹ This is a good point but would benefit from development. The extract does not contain Fred's invitation to Christmas dinner.

❺ Another potentially good point – about Fred's appreciation of the religious as well as the social value of Christmas – is under-developed.

❻ This point is off-focus – it is an important point but not made relevant to Fred's cheerful character.

❼ Kindness is not the same as 'cheerfulness', nor is Fred's greeting to Bob a part of the printed passage, which makes it irrelevant to this part of the answer.

Examiner's comments

Many of the observations are accurate, but they are only occasionally made relevant to the focus of the question. Text is used but not always in support of relevant detail. There is an awareness of the writer making choices, but these are not explicitly linked to the presentation of cheerful characters.

Sample answer 2: a strong answer

Here is an extract from a student response to this question, with the examiner's annotations and final comments. It receives high marks.

The first method that Dickens uses to present Fred's cheerful character is surprise. (1) Knowing Scrooge was a man whom 'nobody' met 'with gladsome looks', the reader suddenly hears a joyous 'A merry Christmas, uncle!' from Scrooge's nephew, Fred. As this is 'the first intimation' of Fred's approach, we, like Scrooge, are taken by surprise.

> (1) Immediate focus on the demand of the question; the idea of 'surprise' as a writer's method is a valid point.

The narrator's second method is to describe Fred's physical appearance, 'all in a glow', 'ruddy and handsome', whose 'eyes sparkled', so that Fred seems, to the reader, to radiate cheerfulness through heat and light. (2)

> (2) Maintains focus on 'method' and offers an insightful comment about Fred's appearance in relation to the question.

In response to Scrooge's declaration of 'Humbug!', Fred, not at all discouraged, engages in an attempt to jolly Scrooge out of his temper, by insisting, cheerfully, 'You don't mean that, I am sure?' (3) Fred replies to Scrooge's accusation – that Fred has no right 'to be merry' as he is 'poor enough' – by wittily questioning Scrooge's right 'to be dismal', concluding 'You're rich enough'. The fact that this was uttered 'gaily', shows Fred maintaining his cheerfulness even when under attack. (4) Fred's cheerful character persists, coaxing Scrooge, in a 'role reversal', appearing to be the more adult of the two, saying, 'Don't be cross, uncle!' (5)

> (3) Well-focused and supported

> (4) Another good example linked to the text

> (5) A perceptive point about the relationship between Scrooge and Fred

Continued

10 Fred

Dickens' most powerful method of presenting Fred's cheerful character here, is seen in his response to Scrooge's comment, 'Much good may it (Christmas) do you! Much good it has ever done you!'. Fred patiently dismisses Scrooge's evaluation of everything in life in terms of 'profit and loss'. Dickens gives Fred a string of positive adjectives – 'good', 'kind', 'forgiving', 'charitable', 'pleasant' – to describe 'Christmas time', appraising it cheerfully as the time when people 'open their shut-up hearts'. 6

6 A good language point linked to the question's demand

Fred ends his tribute to Christmas in an assertively cheerful way: earning a round of applause from Bob Cratchit and fulsome appreciation of Fred's unperturbable cheerfulness from the reader. 7

7 Bob's applause is just outside the scope of the extract, but this is a valid point and brings the section to a neat conclusion.

Examiner's comments

This is an assured response to the question which is well-supported and focused consistently on the presentation of Fred's cheerful character. Methods are analysed and explained clearly, and text is used appropriately.

EXAM TIP

Remember that to achieve the higher levels, everything in your answer should be directly relevant to the specific demands of the question asked.

Retrieval

10

Answer the questions below. Cover the answers column with a piece of paper and write down as many as you can. Check and repeat.

	Questions	Answers
1	Name two of Fred's physical qualities, as described by Dickens.	Two from: 'all in a glow' / 'ruddy face' / 'handsome face' / 'a cheerful voice'
2	Name two benefits of Christmas that Fred lists in his speech to Scrooge in Stave I.	Two from: it is '"a kind, forgiving, charitable, pleasant time…"' / it is a time '"when men and women seem […] to open their shut-up hearts freely"' / it is a time for people '"to think of people below them as if they really were fellow-passengers to the grave"'
3	Complete the quotation: '"the same chance every year, whether he likes it or not, ___ _ ___ ___."'	'"the same chance every year, whether he likes it or not, for I pity him."'
4	Name two things Fred offers Bob Cratchit when he hears of the loss of Tiny Tim.	Two from: his condolences / his service / his card
5	Name three of Fred's functions in the story.	Three from: a foil to Scrooge / embodies Christmas spirit / represents the middle class / Scrooge's connection to family / a role model for Scrooge as an example of social responsibility

Put paper here

Previous questions

Now go back and use these questions to check your knowledge of previous topics.

	Questions	Answers
1	What two childlike activities does Dickens say that Bob takes part in?	Going down a slide, twenty times; rushing home to play 'blindman's-buff'
2	Complete the quotation: 'The clerk in the ____ involuntarily ________.'	'The clerk in the tank involuntarily applauded.'
3	When Mrs Cratchit objects to Bob's toast to Scrooge as the 'Founder of the Feast', how does Bob calm her down?	By reminding her of the presence of the children and that it is Christmas time
4	How much does Bob earn as clerk to Scrooge?	Fifteen shillings per week
5	To which character does Bob function as a foil?	Scrooge

Put paper here

Now turn to page 103 and complete Practice question 2.

Knowledge CHARACTERS

11 The Ghost of Jacob Marley

The presentation of the Ghost of Jacob Marley

Marley's Ghost appears in Stave I and is referred to at the start of Staves II, III and V, and the end of Stave III. There is no mention of the character in Stave IV.

Method of presentation	What this reveals about the Ghost of Jacob Marley
Marley's appearance/ qualities	• Marley's face appears first, when Scrooge's door knocker 'morphs' into it: it 'was not angry or ferocious [...] with ghostly spectacles turned up on its ghostly forehead. The hair was curiously stirred [...] and, though the eyes were wide open, they were perfectly motionless.' • Later, Marley's whole 'body' appears: 'in his pigtail, usual waistcoat, tights and boots [...] The chain he drew was clasped about his middle [...] His body was transparent'.
What Marley does	• Marley regrets his past life – entirely focused on money and profit, like Scrooge – and leads his ghost to try to save Scrooge, 'his sole friend', from suffering his own fate – 'doomed to wander through the world [...] and witness what it cannot share.' • Marley's Ghost sends the three Spirits to 'haunt' Scrooge, giving him a chance to alter his life – and his after-life – for the better.
What Marley says	• Marley's Ghost's message to Scrooge is urgent and deeply felt: '"I am here to-night to warn you, that you have yet a chance and hope of escaping my fate."' • He explains to Scrooge: '"I wear the chain I forged in life [...] I girded it on of my own free will, and of my own free will I wore it. Is its pattern strange to *you*?"' • Marley's Ghost tells Scrooge he is adding to a 'ponderous chain' of his own and that without the visit from the three Spirits Scrooge cannot avoid '"the path I tread"'. This introduces the idea that Scrooge, too, must 'follow a path' that will lead to a better outcome.
What others think or say about Marley	• At first, Scrooge cannot believe in Marley's Ghost, suggesting it might be a symptom of indigestion: '"You may be an undigested bit of beef [...] There's more of gravy than of grave about you."" • He calls Marley '"a good man of business"' but Marley's Ghost scoffs at him, insisting, '"Mankind was my business. The common welfare was my business; charity, mercy, forbearance, and benevolence, were, all, my business."'

Method of presentation	What this reveals about the Ghost of Jacob Marley
How Marley compares/contrasts with other characters	• Marley's Ghost is directly compared to Scrooge. Although their relationship was as business partners, there is a suggestion that they were platonic 'soul mates' as they each spent their lives pursuing profit.
How Marley expresses himself	• Marley's Ghost speaks in an 'other-worldly' style. Scrooge begs him, '"Don't be flowery, Jacob!"' but Marley persists in speaking in a formal, **stilted** way, appropriate for someone 'beyond the grave' with deeper knowledge of 'life and death' than mere mortals: '"Why did I walk through crowds of fellow-beings with my eyes turned down, and never raise them to that blessed Star which led the Wise Men to a poor abode!"'

Function

- Serves as a warning to Scrooge – Marley serves as a warning to Scrooge about what will await him if he does not change.
- Represents the consequences of greed – Marley's chains symbolise the cost of living a life focused on money and greed.
- Shows of the importance of making good choices – Marley's character could serve to remind readers to reflect on their actions and change themselves for the better.
- Demonstrates the importance of remorse and redemption – Marley highlights the importance of change and repentance, key themes in the story.

Key terms Make sure you can write a definition for this key term

stilted

Retrieval

Answer the questions below. Cover the answers column with a piece of paper and write down as many as you can. Check and repeat.

	Questions	Answers
1	Which part of Marley's Ghost is first to appear and where does Scrooge see it?	His face; in his doorknocker
2	What emotion does Marley feel, looking back on his life?	Regret
3	Complete the quotation '"I wear the chain I ______ in life [...] I made it ____ ____ ____, and yard by yard."'	'"I wear the chain I forged in life [...] I made it link by link, and yard by yard."'
4	How does Scrooge react to Marley's Ghost at first?	In disbelief – he thinks it may be a symptom of indigestion
5	How does Marley's Ghost react to Scrooge's compliment that he was a 'good man of business'?	He scoffs and insists that 'Mankind' was his business
6	Name three aspects of life that Marley's Ghost insists were really his business in life.	Three from: mankind / the common welfare / charity / mercy / forbearance / benevolence

Put paper here

Previous questions

Use the questions below to check your knowledge from previous chapters.

	Questions	Answers
1	Name two of Fred's physical qualities as described by Dickens.	Two from: 'all in a glow' features / 'ruddy face' / 'handsome face' / 'a cheerful voice'
2	Name two benefits of Christmas that Fred lists in his speech to Scrooge in Stave I.	Two from: it is '"a kind, forgiving, charitable, pleasant time..."' / it is a time '"when men and women seem [...] to open their shut-up hearts freely"' / it is a time for people '"to think of people below them as if they really were fellow-passengers to the grave"'
3	Complete the quotation: '"the same chance every year, whether he likes it or not, ______ ______ ______ ______."'	'"the same chance every year, whether he likes it or not, for I pity him."'
4	Name two things Fred offers Bob Cratchit when he hears of the loss of Tiny Tim.	Two from: his condolences / his service / his card

Put paper here

Now turn to page 104 and complete Practice question 3.

12 The Ghosts of Christmas Past, Present, and Yet to Come

The three Spirits

The three Spirits

- Each spirit appears in one stave only: the Ghost of Christmas Past in Stave II, the Ghost of Christmas Present in Stave III, and the Ghost of Christmas Yet to Come in Stave IV (although he makes his initial appearance at the very end of Stave III).
- Only Scrooge experiences the Spirits. While he learns from each of them, he makes no comment on any of them.
- The Spirits contrast with one another in their distinctive styles of guiding Scrooge, but their aims are identical in wishing to bring about his self-discovery and salvation.

The qualities of the three Spirits

The Spirits may be seen as three different aspects of the mind: memory, perception, and fears and imaginings. For example, the light from the Spirit of Christmas Past represents memory. Some of Scrooge's memories – like those of Fezziwig – are bright, while his memory of Belle releasing him from their engagement is too dark to bear.

Ghost of Christmas Past represents memory	Ghost of Christmas Present represents perception	Ghost of Christmas Yet to Come represents fears and imaginings
'like a child […] like an old man [...] Its hair […] white as if with age […] the face had not a wrinkle […] wore a tunic of the purest white […] from the crown of its head there sprung a […] jet of light […] its belt sparkled […] now in one part and now in another […] what was light one instant, at another time was dark'	'clothed in one simple green robe […] its […] breast was bare, as if disdaining […] artifice. Its feet […] were also bare; and on its head …] a holly wreath, set […] with shining icicles. Its dark brown curls were long and free; free as its genial face, its sparkling eye, its open hand, its cheery voice […] its joyful air.'	'It was shrouded in a deep black garment, which concealed its head, its face, its form, and left nothing of it visible save one outstretched hand. But for this it would have been difficult to detach its figure from the night […] the darkness by which it was surrounded.'

Knowledge CHARACTERS

12 The Ghosts of Christmas Past, Present, and Yet to Come

The actions of the three Spirits

Ghost of Christmas Past	Ghost of Christmas Present	Ghost of Christmas Yet to Come
• Guides Scrooge through memories from his childhood, youth and more mature years. • Some memories are brighter than others, and some Scrooge does not wish to face.	• Takes Scrooge to see different people celebrating Christmas; including the poor, but loving, Cratchit family; Fred's rich, but equally amiable, friends and family; miners, lighthouse men, and sailors. • Sets Scrooge straight on a few of his misconceptions and gives him an unambiguous answer to his question about Tiny Tim. • Enlightens Scrooge about the dangers of ignorance and want.	• Shows Scrooge what may occur in the future, unless Scrooge changes. • Inspires Scrooge to ask to see someone who feels 'emotion' at the death of the unknown man, and then to request a glimpse of tenderness towards a death. • Reveals Scrooge's gravestone – the final impetus towards Scrooge's redemption.

What the three Spirits say

Ghost of Christmas Past	Ghost of Christmas Present	Ghost of Christmas Yet to Come
• Encourages Scrooge to take a close look at himself. When Scrooge inquires '"what business brought him there"', it replies, '"Your welfare!"' • Observes it is '"Strange to have forgotten it for so many years!"' when Scrooge claims great familiarity with the 'open country road' he shows him first. • Makes Scrooge 'uneasy' by reminding him that Fred is the child of Fan; quizzes Scrooge over his desire to speak to his clerk after seeing Fezziwig; insists on showing him 'One shadow more' when the thought of losing Belle has become unbearable to Scrooge.	• More emphatic than the others, responding to Scrooge's enjoyment of Fred's party with pleasure. • Tells Scrooge of the '"vacant seat"' that Tim will leave if the future is '"unaltered"' and reminds Scrooge of his cruel solution to the '"surplus population"'. • He also tells him bluntly: '"It may be, that in the sight of Heaven, you are more worthless and less fit to live than millions like this poor man's child."'	• The most unsettling to Scrooge; he deals in what might be rather than what 'was' or 'is'. • Because he says nothing, Scrooge must imagine the meaning of what he experiences in this Spirit's presence.

How the three Spirits convey their messages

Ghost of Christmas Past	Ghost of Christmas Present	Ghost of Christmas Yet to Come
Kindly but formally reminding Scrooge of his past; stimulating his memory.	Cheerfully yet clearly conveying his message.	Ominously silent, encouraging Scrooge to imagine his meaning.

Function

- Help Scrooge to learn – The spirits help Scrooge learn about himself and how to change his ways.
- Show Scrooge the consequences of his behaviour – The spirits show Scrooge what will happen if he continues with his current actions and attitudes.
- As a reminder of mortality – The spirits remind Scrooge of his own mortality and what will be thought of him after his death. This reminder could also be heeded by the reader.
- Remind Scrooge of his past – The Ghost of Christmas Past reminds Scrooge that he wasn't always bitter and greedy.
- Show Scrooge positive examples – The Ghost of Christmas Present shows Scrooge examples of generosity and goodwill, and the importance of Christmas spirit and family.
- Reveal Scrooge's possible future – The Ghost of Christmas Yet to Come reveals to Scrooge the consequences if he continues to live a selfish, cruel, and greedy life.

REVISION TIP

When revising characters, begin by looking at the parts of the story they are involved in – their key moments. This will help you think about the ideas that emerge from their actions.

Retrieval

Answer the questions below. Cover the answers column with a piece of paper and write down as many as you can. Check and repeat.

	Questions	Answers
1	What aspect of the mind might the Ghost of Christmas Past represent?	Memory
2	Name three aspects of the physical appearance of the Ghost of Christmas Past.	Three from: 'like a child' / 'like an old man' / 'white hair' / 'unwrinkled face' / 'white tunic' / 'from the crown of its head there sprung a […] jet of light' / 'its belt sparkled'
3	Name three aspects of the physical appearance of the Ghost of Christmas Present.	Three from: 'clothed in one simple green robe' / bare-chested / bare feet / holly wreath on its head / 'dark brown curls were long and free' / 'its genial face / its sparkling eye / its open hand / its cheery voice […] its joyful air.'
4	Name two aspects of the physical appearance of the Ghost of Christmas Yet to Come.	Two from: 'shrouded in a deep black garment' / 'concealed its head, its face, its form' / 'one outstretched hand' / surrounded by darkness
5	What does Scrooge ask the Ghost of Christmas Yet To Come to show him when he witnesses the indifference of others to the dead man's death?	Someone who feels 'emotion' at the death of the unknown man
6	Complete the quotation: '"It may be, that in the sight of Heaven, you are more ________ ___ ___ __ __ ___ than millions like this poor man's child."'	'"It may be, that in the sight of Heaven, you are more <u>worthless</u> <u>and</u> <u>less</u> <u>fit</u> <u>to</u> <u>live</u> than millions like this poor man's child."'
7	How does the Ghost of Christmas Past convey its messages to Scrooge?	Kindly but formally, stimulating his memory
8	How does the Ghost of Christmas Present convey his messages to Scrooge?	Cheerfully, yet clearly
9	How does the Ghost of Christmas Yet to Come convey his messages to Scrooge?	Ominously silently

Put paper here

Previous questions

Now go back and use these questions to check your knowledge of previous topics.

	Questions	Answers
1	Which part of Marley's Ghost is first to appear, and where does Scrooge see it?	His face; in his doorknocker
2	How does Marley's Ghost react to Scrooge's compliment that he was a 'good man of business'?	He scoffs and insists that 'Mankind' was his business

Put paper here

Now turn to page 109 and complete Practice question 7.

13 Other characters

The Cratchits

Method of presentation	What this reveals about the Cratchits
Physical appearances/ qualities	• Mrs Cratchit is described as wearing worn clothes, decorated with cheap ribbons. • Tiny Tim has a disability: 'he bore a little crutch, and had his limbs supported by an iron frame!'
What they do in the story	• Mrs Cratchit is a 'model' wife and mother, she loves Bob and supports him in his grief over Tiny Tim's death. • Tiny Tim goes to church with Bob on Christmas Day and joins in the happy family life of the Cratchits. • Martha and Peter work in decent, if low-paying jobs; aiming to better themselves.
What they say in the story	• Mrs Cratchit speaks harshly of Scrooge: but lovingly of her family. • Tiny Tim is cheerful: '"God bless us every one!" said Tiny Tim.'
Observations of other characters	• Peter reminds Bob that '"Everybody knows"' that Mrs Cratchit is '"a good wife"'. • Bob says Tim has been '"As good as gold […] and better."'
Comparison/ contrast with other characters	• Mrs Cratchit is poor but dignified and may be compared to the laundress and charwoman who steal. • Tiny Tim symbolises both innocence and patience in accepting his situation and may be compared to any of the characters who are less satisfied with what they have, like the thieves. • In contrast to Scrooge's self-imposed solitary existence, the Cratchits are shown in companionable harmony on Christmas Day.
How they express themselves	• Mrs Cratchit's speech is informal and not grammatically correct; but it is not coarse: '"What has ever got your precious father then? [...] And Martha warn't as late last Christmas Day by half-an-hour?"' • We hear little direct speech from Tim but when he does speak, it is invariably cheerful and optimistic. • The children don't say much but all they say shows a happy family, sometimes teasing one another.

Function of the Cratchits

- Representing a working class family – The struggles and challenges faced by the Cratchits highlight the importance of family and the consequences of social inequality.
- Conveying the value of family – Dickens shows the unity, happiness, and joy in the Cratchit family, despite their poverty.
- Reveal consequences of selfishness – The Cratchits show the direct consequences of Scrooge's actions. Scrooge's refusal to pay Bob fairly, means they are unable to provide medical care for Tiny Tim, leading to his death.

REVISION TIP

Never underestimate the contribution made to the story by minor characters. However small a role they play, each one is part of Dickens' design to show Scrooge's transformation into a 'good' man.

13 Other characters

Characters shown by the Ghost of Christmas Past

Young Scrooge	Fezziwig	Belle
• Scrooge is shown a vision of himself, as a young boy, 'neglected by his friends'; his only company are 'fictional' characters. • Young Scrooge's reunion with his beloved sister, Fan, and the Ghost's reminder of her 'large heart', which Scrooge remembers makes him 'uneasy' because of his coldness to Fred, Fan's only son.	• Fezziwig is a respectful and generous employer, shaking hands and wishing his workers 'a Merry Christmas' one by one. The Fezziwigs join with them in dancing and feasting to celebrate the spirit of Christmas and to spread good will. • Scrooge concludes that the happiness that Fezziwig brought was '"as great as if it cost a fortune"' prompting him to wish he could '"say a word or two"' to his clerk, and to regret that he can't do so.	• Belle (meaning 'beautiful'), who is Scrooge's former fiancée, reveals Scrooge's capacity for love, as a young man, that has been destroyed by his obsession: 'Gain'. • The Ghost insists that Scrooge faces up to what he lost when Belle broke off their engagement. He shows Scrooge a scene, that might have been his, had he married Belle and had his own family to love. The vision is so painful to Scrooge that he attempts to put out the Spirit's 'light'.

Function of characters shown by the Ghost of Christmas Past

All of these characters from Scrooge's past remind Scrooge – and inform the reader – of tender emotions that Scrooge was once capable of: loneliness, joy, gratitude, and love.

REVISION TIP

With more minor characters, it is important to look closely at their relationship with main characters – how their words and actions have influence, and how their values and conduct contrast with those of main characters.

Characters shown by the Ghost of Christmas Present

Characters at Fred's Christmas party	'Ignorance' and 'Want'
• Fred's wife – called 'Scrooge's niece' throughout – is described positively: 'She was very pretty […] With a dimpled, surprised-looking, capital face; a ripe little mouth, that seemed made to be kissed […] and the sunniest pair of eyes you ever saw…'. Like Fred, she is presented as amiable and welcoming. She is more critical of Scrooge than Fred is, declaring herself to '"have no patience"' with him, but without any resentment. • Topper and the 'plump sister', like Fred and his wife, are part of the middle class in society, living comfortably and enjoying sharing their Christmas with friends and family. Dickens makes no criticism of people who have money, only of those for whom 'getting' money is their sole aim in life.	• The Ghost of Christmas Present is the jolliest of all the Spirits, so it is shocking when he reveals two 'wretched children' described as: 'Yellow, meagre, ragged, scowling, wolfish…' from beneath his robes and explains that they represent ignorance and want. • These children symbolise the millions of people who live in poverty and ignorance in the world and whom Scrooge originally believed should be sent to prisons and workhouses.

Function of characters shown by the Ghost of Christmas Present

- Fred's party guests rejuvenate Scrooge, helping him to appreciate the value of friends and family and embodying Dickens' ideas about Christmas spirit.
- 'Ignorance' and 'Want' are a powerful reminder of Scrooge's earlier indifference to the sufferings of others and the consequences of social inequality.

REMEMBER

Unlike the rest of the characters (apart from the Spirits) who are presented realistically, the 'children' Ignorance and Want are entirely symbolic and intended to represent those living in poverty and ignorance.

Knowledge CHARACTERS

13 Other characters

Characters shown by the Ghost of Christmas Yet to Come

Businessmen in the city	Old Joe, three thieves, debtors
They show Scrooge their indifference to his 'death' and their contempt for him.	They show Scrooge their relief at his death and satisfaction at having benefited financially.
Like Scrooge, at the beginning of the novel, they represent the 'unfeeling' rich.	They represent the 'undeserving poor'.
Presented in ways that Dickens deemed to be negative, both physically and through their words and actions: • 'A great fat man with a monstrous chin' • A man 'taking a vast quantity of snuff' • 'a red-faced gentleman with a pendulous excrescence on the end of his nose, that shook like the gills of a turkey-cock'. • They joke about Scrooge's death, his likely 'cheap funeral' and their unwillingness to attend it without the prospect of a lunch. • Others refer to Scrooge as 'old Scratch' before moving swiftly onto the subject of the weather.	• Old Joe – 'was a grey-haired rascal, nearly seventy years of age'. • Mrs Dilber, the laundress, the unnamed charwoman and the undertaker are not described physically. They are presented as a group of shameless and grasping individuals, who are actually proud of profiting from the death of the '"wicked old screw"'. The charwoman boasts of having stolen his bedcurtains by taking '"'em down, rings and all, with him lying there…"'. • Caroline, a young mother, and her 'careworn and depressed' young husband, who owe Scrooge money that they are unable to pay are also delighted by the death of '"so merciless a creditor"'.

Function of characters shown by the Ghost of Christmas Yet to Come

Many of the characters that Scrooge observes here are unnamed commentators on Scrooge's 'death'. Taken as a whole, these characters are important in bringing Scrooge into a state of understanding of what others think of him, and therefore in helping him to decide to be a 'better man'.

- These characters illustrate the problems of debt and poverty.
- They also help to show that it is important to use money to do good. They demonstrate that Scrooge's money will be of no use to him when he is dead. This conveys Dickens' idea that wealth should be used to help others.

REVISION TIP

When writing about minor characters, try to show the precise effect that each one has on Scrooge. Some teach him how to behave well to others while others teach him that greed and selfishness lead to misery.

Retrieval

Answer the questions below. Cover the answers column with a piece of paper and write down as many as you can. Check and repeat.

	Questions	Answers
1	Name an aspect of Mrs Cratchit's appearance on Christmas Day.	One from: worn clothes / cheap ribbons
2	Give two examples of words that Mrs Cratchit uses to describe Scrooge.	Two from: 'odious' / 'stingy' / 'hard' / 'unfeeling'
3	What other two women in the story provide a contrast to good Mrs Cratchit?	Charwoman; laundress
4	How does the Cratchit family contrast with Scrooge?	Scrooge's 'solitary existence' contrasts with their 'companionable harmony'
5	Who is Belle?	Scrooge's former fiancée
6	Complete the quotation: Scrooge tells the Ghost that the happiness that Fezziwig brought was '"as great as if it ____ _ _______."'	"as great as if it cost a fortune."
7	What emotions do the characters from Scrooge's past remind Scrooge – and inform the reader – of?	Loneliness; joy; gratitude, love
8	Dickens is critical of people who have money. True or false?	False – he is only critical of people for whom 'getting' money is their sole aim in life
9	Name two of the characters who represent the 'undeserving poor'.	Two from: Old Joe / laundress / charwoman

Put paper here

Previous questions

Now go back and use these questions to check your knowledge of previous topics.

	Questions	Answers
1	What aspect of the mind might the Ghost of Christmas Past represent?	Memory
2	What emotion does Marley feel, looking back on his life?	Regret
3	How does Scrooge react to Marley's Ghost at first?	In disbelief – he thinks it may be a symptom of indigestion

Put paper here

Now turn to page 122 and complete Practice question 17.

Knowledge THEMES

14 Redemption

Themes and ways of presenting them

The ideas of a text – what the text is 'about' – are sometimes called 'themes'. When you study a text, the events and characters' actions combine to reveal ideas and themes. In *A Christmas Carol*, themes are presented in many ways, including:

- the title
- the plot
- direct address by the narrator
- characters acting as mouthpieces for the author's views on themes
- characters discussing themes
- characters representing themes through their actions
- repeated motifs, symbols, and images
- one or more themes presented together or as a contrast to one another.

REMEMBER

In an exam question, themes may be referred to using different words or terms from those you have revised. If you don't recognise the theme in the question, take a pause, and see if it is actually the same as, or very close to, one of the themes that you have revised. For example:

- redemption is similar in meaning to reclamation, salvation, or enlightenment
- the theme of poverty and the poor may appear as 'social injustice' or 'rich and poor'
- the theme of Christmas spirit may be referred to in relation to charity or goodwill.

How redemption is presented

Commentaries on *A Christmas Carol* sometimes refer to themes of 'salvation' or 'redemption'. Both terms are associated with Christianity and refer to the saving of a person's 'soul'. Dickens does not use either of these words explicitly in the text. However, the Ghost of Christmas Past tells Scrooge that one reason for his visit is: '"Your **reclamation**"'. Reclamation implies that Scrooge may recover better qualities that he has lost, over time.

Plot

We learn that Scrooge was once a vulnerable child, an enthusiastic and willing apprentice, engaged to marry Belle, a good man with 'nobler aspirations'. Belle says: '"I have seen your nobler aspirations fall off one by one"'

We learn that Scrooge has been hardened by a love of money, a fear of poverty, years working with Marley, when Marley put 'business' before '"charity, mercy [...] and benevolence"'.

The Ghost of Christmas Past says 'his business' is Scrooge's 'reclamation'. It shows Scrooge visions of his former, better self, to inspire him to recover, reclaim, and redeem these aspects of his character.

REVISION TIP

Plot a graph of the moments when Scrooge feels some emotion as he watches the 'visions'.

Direct address

Having originally described Scrooge negatively in Stave I:

'Hard and sharp as flint [...] secret, and self-contained, and solitary as an oyster,'

the narrator tells us directly about Scrooge's redemption in Stave V:

'He became as good a friend, as good a master, and as good a man, as the good old city knew'

Characters discussing redemption

Fred discusses Scrooge's potential redemption when he explains to his party guests his intended strategy for helping Scrooge:

'"I mean to give him the same chance every year [...] for I pity him. He may rail at Christmas till he dies, but he can't help thinking better of it [...] if he finds me going there, in good temper, year after year [...] saying Uncle Scrooge, how are you?"'

Characters' actions

Scrooge, in being 'reclaimed', actually 'does' the theme. When presented with his own tombstone, Scrooge begs the Ghost of Christmas Yet to Come that he be allowed to learn from the lessons the Spirits have taught him:

'"Oh, tell me I may sponge away the writing on this stone!"'

Repeated motifs, symbols, and images

Dickens uses repeated motifs and images of the weather, light and warmth to show Scrooge's redemption from a state of spiritual darkness:

'It was cold, bleak, biting weather; foggy withal [...] it had not been light all day'

In Stave V, Scrooge, reclaimed, wakes to 'glorious' winter weather:

'No fog, no mist; clear, bright, jovial [...] Golden sunlight; Heavenly sky'

Five key points about redemption

1. The ghosts help Scrooge to rediscover the qualities of his youth, recognise the error of his ways, and change for the better.
2. Dickens shows Scrooge's transformation as an example to readers, who should examine their own behaviour and embrace the qualities of Christmas spirit as Scrooge does.
3. The narrator pinpoints moments when Scrooge begins to feel emotions such as empathy again.
4. Dickens uses images of light and dark, warmth and cold, to chart Scrooge's progress.
5. Bob and Fred are each 'good' men who act as 'models' for Scrooge's redemption.

Key terms Make sure you can write a definition for these key term

reclamation

14 Redemption

Writing about redemption

Sample answer 1: not a strong answer

Here is an extract from a student response to this question, with the examiner's annotations and final comments. It receives less than half marks.

Extract from Stave IV, from: '"Before I draw nearer to that stone to which you point," said Scrooge, "answer me one question."' to: '... It shrunk, collapsed, and dwindled down into a bedpost.'

> Starting with this extract, explore how Dickens presents the theme of Scrooge's redemption in *A Christmas Carol.* **[30 marks]**

The theme of redemption is very important in 'A Christmas Carol'. Scrooge changes from a mean old man who cares for nobody, to a pillar of society. ❶ He does this through his meetings with three Spirits sent by the ghost Jacob Marley. Marley's Ghost terrifies Scrooge out of his wits ❷ by appearing in his room weighed down by chains and shows Scrooge that living to make money means suffering after death. ❸ Scrooge does not want to be haunted but agrees because Marley's Ghost explains how long Scrooge's chain is now. Marley describes it as a 'ponderous chain'. ❹ The first two Spirits are friendly with Scrooge and show him his past and his present. The last Spirit, of Christmas Yet to Come, is very scary. In this passage, he shows Scrooge his own grave, which freaks him out and he promises to change his ways. ❺ In the next chapter Scrooge calls out cheerfully to a boy and sends him to buy a turkey for Bob Cratchit. He even pays for a cab for the boy – this is a huge change for Scrooge who, in the first stave, chased away a ragged carol-singer because of his humbug attitude to Christmas. ❻ When Scrooge is with the Spirits they show him things that he might have done better, like not breaking up with Belle and not working on the day Marley was buried. ❼

❶ This is a straightforward but effective introduction which offers a focused and succinct summary.

❷ This is not strictly accurate. An appropriate quotation from Stave I might have been more helpful here.

❸ Evidence of understanding here

❹ This quotation is apt but not explored and explained in reference to the question.

❺ The student only briefly covers a lot of events before making a comment on the printed passage. The phrase 'freaks him out' is too casual for an exam answer.

❻ This paragraph has some relevance to the question but it is under-developed. The use of 'humbug', as an adjective, suggests a lack of full understanding of its meaning.

❼ The reference to Scrooge's experience of what he might have done better in life is relevant but not explored in terms of the theme of redemption.

8 Scrooge's enjoyment of the party implies some change in Scrooge but it has not been made explicit.

He even begs the Spirit to let him stay at Fred's party because he is enjoying the games which he thought would be humbug before. 8

Examiner's comments

There are some accurate and straightforward points made about Scrooge's redemption. The candidate identifies a few moments from the story which could be explored in more detail; there are some supported references to moments in the text. However, focus on Dickens' methods of presenting the theme of redemption is limited.

Sample answer 2: a strong answer

Here is an extract from a student response to this question, with the examiner's annotations and final comments. It receives high marks.

'A Christmas Carol' might easily be subtitled: 'The Redemption of Ebenezer Scrooge', since that is the focus of the story. 1 *Dickens' main method of presenting this theme is through the plot and Scrooge's 'journey' to becoming 'as good a man' as any. This extract occurs at the point of Scrooge's realisation that he must take his chance now if he is to avoid the fate of Jacob Marley.* 2

1 Good focus on the question

2 Clear focus on Dickens' method of presenting the theme and useful reference to the significance of this passage for Scrooge's future

The Ghosts offer Scrooge an educational tour of his past and potential future. Scrooge is a mere 'bystander' to the events he sees, but his reactions to them result in his 'reclamation'. 3 *Scrooge accepts Marley's offer of a 'hope' of escaping his own fate; he gains the 'chance' to reject 'isolation', re-join society and 'interfere, for good, in human matters'. He embarks, with some reluctance, on a spiritual journey.* 4

3 This is a succinct summary of Scrooge's experience with the Ghosts.

4 Good choice of brief references reveals a secure knowledge of the text, and focus on redemption

The Ghost of Christmas Past shows Scrooge the qualities that he once had and that he may reclaim. 5

5 Good understanding of the significance of the term 'redemption' in relation to Scrooge

Continued

14 Redemption

Scrooge sees the joy of his younger self. He sees his vulnerability, forgotten by his family at Christmas; his enthusiasm for the fictional characters who kept him 'company'; the love he had for his little sister, Fan. Scrooge's 'hard' heart begins to soften. ❻ Scrooge rediscovers his zest for fun at Fezziwig's Christmas party, and he recognises the value of an employer's generous spirit. The Ghost's 'visions' awaken Scrooge's conscience about the carol-singer he had chased away and his shabby treatment of his clerk. Scrooge finds the memory of Belle unbearable, seeing his former self through her loving eyes, and accepting her judgement on his moral decline. ❼ Scrooge hears what others think about his 'present' self in Stave III. Dickens implies that he reflects on their opinions. The Ghost allows him to see how others 'keep' their Christmases and how, without fail, Christmas does them 'good'. ❽ Scrooge realises that the dreadful future predicted for him may only be avoided through a return to the joy, vulnerability, enthusiasm, and noble principles of his youth. ❾ In Stave V, Dickens once more relies upon imagery of light and sounds to emphasise the joy of Scrooge's redemption. No longer 'cold and bleak', Scrooge's life is bathed in golden sunlight' and the 'glorious' sounds of 'merry bells'. Dickens shows how Scrooge awakens, on Christmas morning, under a 'heavenly sky', renewed and redeemed. ❿

❻ Useful summary of Scrooge's qualities as a younger man

❼ Consistently focused on the qualities that Scrooge 'redeems' thanks to his experiences with the Spirits

❽ Concise points are made about the effects on Scrooge of his time spent with the Ghost of Christmas Present.

❾ Mentions Scrooge's realisation in the passage of how he needs to change to avoid the 'predictions' of the Ghost of Christmas Yet to Come

❿ Exploration of Dickens' use of imagery, fully focused on meeting the brief of the question

Examiner's comments

This is a succinct and well-structured answer. It takes a thoughtful approach to the task and to selected moments from the novel as a whole, supported by a range of appropriate references. There is useful analysis of some of Dickens' methods of presenting Scrooge's change. A convincing exploration of the theme of redemption.

Retrieval

Answer the questions below. Cover the answers column with a piece of paper and write down as many as you can. Check and repeat.

	Questions	Answers
1	The term 'redemption' is another way of expressing 'reclamation' or 'salvation'. True or false?	True
2	Which of the three Ghosts of Christmas tells Scrooge that their business with him is his 'reclamation'?	The Ghost of Christmas Past
3	What does the redemption of Scrooge result in?	Scrooge recovers some of the better qualities from his younger days that he had lost
4	Complete the quotation: 'He became as good a _____, as good a ______, and as good a ____, as the good old city knew'.	'He became as good a friend, as good a master, and as good a man, as the good old city knew'.
5	Who wishes to give Scrooge the same chance every year to recover his better self, because he pities him?	Fred
6	Complete the quotation: '"Oh, tell me I may _______ _____ the writing on this stone!"'	'"Oh, tell me I may sponge away the writing on this stone!"'
7	Complete the quotation: 'No fog, no ____; clear, bright, _____'	'No fog, no mist; clear, bright, jovial'
8	Name two motifs or images that Dickens uses to show Scrooge's progress.	Two from: light / dark / warmth / cold
9	Which two characters act as models for Scrooge's redemption?	Bob; Fred

Put paper here

Previous questions

Now go back and use these questions to check your knowledge of previous topics.

	Questions	Answers
1	Who is Belle?	Scrooge's former fiancée
2	Dickens is critical of people who have money. True or false?	False – he is only critical of people for whom 'getting' money is their sole aim in life
3	Name any two of the characters who represent the 'undeserving poor'.	Two from: Old Joe / laundress / charwoman

Put paper here

Now turn to page 118 and complete Practice question 14.

Knowledge THEMES

15 Poverty and social inequality

How poverty and social inequality are presented

Plot

The theme is highlighted throughout the plot as Scrooge's redemption is partly defined in terms of his change of attitude towards the poor. His attitude in the beginning is mainly indifference:

'"If they would rather die," […] "they had better do it, and decrease the surplus population."'

Scrooge sees evidence of social inequality in Bob Cratchit's home, where Bob's weekly wage is not enough to cover medical help for Tiny Tim. He is told by the Spirit that without intervention, Tiny Tim will die:

'"If these shadows remain unaltered by the Future, the child will die."'

Direct address

In Stave I, the narrator highlights social inequality by telling us of a group of poor folk, huddled round a workmen's fire for warmth, on Christmas Eve.

'a great fire […] round which a party of ragged men and boys were gathered: warming their hands'

In Stave IV, the narrator describes the poverty in the city streets, where the three thieves exchange the items stolen from the 'dead man' for cash: this suggests a place where some of the most 'wretched' poor exist.

'The ways were foul […] the shops and houses wretched; the people half-naked, drunken, slipshod, ugly […] and the whole quarter reeked with crime, with filth, and misery.'

Characters acting as mouthpieces

Dickens uses the 'portly gentlemen' to act as a mouthpiece for his own views on the poor and social injustices.

'"we should make some slight provision for the Poor and destitute […]. Many […] are in want of common comforts"'

Characters discussing themes

In addition to the 'portly gentlemen' discussing the needs of the poor, Marley's Ghost talks of their sufferings and insists upon the obligation of every right-thinking citizen to make it their 'business' to help them.

'"Mankind was my business. […] Were there no poor homes to which its light would have conducted *me*?"'

Characters representing poverty

Living in a rented 'four-roomed house' as a family of eight, the Cratchits represent the 'deserving poor'.

'They were not a handsome family; […] But they were happy, grateful, pleased […] and contented'

The laundress and charwoman represent the 'undeserving poor'; they are cast as thieves.

Repeated motifs, symbols, and images

The theme of poverty is also presented through symbolism when the Ghost of Christmas Present reveals the girl, Want, and the boy, Ignorance, from under his garments. 'Want' and 'Ignorance' are both the products of social injustice, victims of a society that favoured the wealthy and made inadequate provision for the poor.

'From the foldings of its robe it brought two children; wretched, abject, frightful, hideous, miserable.'

Pairing with other themes

Wealth and poverty are contrasting themes. Scrooge calls Fred 'poor', despite his fine house and lavish parties. Fred is only 'poor' in not having as much money as Scrooge – he certainly does not live in poverty!

Fred calls Scrooge 'rich' in response:

Scrooge: '"What right have you to be merry? What reason have you to be merry? You're poor enough."'

Fred: '"What right have you to be dismal? What reason have you to be morose? You're rich enough."'

REVISION TIP

Ideas and themes develop during the course of a story – new events and characters' decisions add further layers to a theme. Look for key moments in a story where something significant happens that adds to a theme.

Five key points about poverty and social inequality

1. At first, Scrooge has contempt for the poor and thinks them idle and worthless.
2. Seeing the 'surplus population', close-up, in ailing Tiny Tim, Scrooge feels ashamed.
3. Dickens uses the Cratchit family to show the consequences of social inequality and convey his ideas about social justice and kindness to others.
4. Dickens contrasts Scrooge with other characters to show that accumulation of wealth does not bring joy.
5. Scrooge's reintegration into 'society' highlights the benefits of 'sharing' wealth around.

REVISION TIP

Make a flow chart of each time Scrooge meets representatives of the 'poor' (such as the unnamed carol singer in Stave I) and how he reacts in each case.

15 Poverty and social inequality

Writing about poverty and social inequality

Sample answer 1: not a strong answer

Here is an extract from a student response to this question, with the examiner's annotations and final comments. It receives less than half marks.

> Starting with this extract, explore how Dickens presents social inequality in *A Christmas Carol*.
>
> **[30 marks]**

Dickens shows us the rich and the poor in 'A Christmas Carol'. In this passage, Bob Cratchit's home is visited by the wealthy (miserly) Scrooge and a Spirit. These 'guests' observe a 'poor' man's traditional Christmas dinner served with lashings of love. ❶ Dickens shows that Scrooge is strongly affected by the scene. ❷ In Scrooge's journey towards redemption, this is a turning point. Scrooge will go on to see other poor homes and working-class people. They are part of the social fabric that the wealthy classes depend upon but who Dickens shows, through Scrooge, they care little for. ❸ In visiting Bob Cratchit, Scrooge is made aware of the home life of his humble clerk who he treats so badly. ❹ Later, Scrooge sees how other workers, equally badly treated, celebrate Christmas despite their low position in society. ❺ Dickens suggests that the rich take the poor for granted – if they are injured or can no longer work, their shocking view would be: '"What then? If he be like to die, he had better do it, and decrease the surplus population."' ❻

❶ This identifies the immediate context of the extract.

❷ Still confident and relevant

❸ This is a useful reference to Dicken's wider purpose in the novel.

❹ A relevant observation

❺ Good point

❻ The student concludes this part of the answer with an apt quotation from the passage which is relevant to the issue of social inequality.

Examiner's comments

This answer shows a grasp of Dickens' intentions in *A Christmas Carol*, revealing an understanding of the social context whereby the wealthy members of society depend upon the working classes for their comforts in life. Understanding of the theme that is the focus of the question is demonstrated. The work is thoughtful but lacks detailed support.

Sample answer 2: a strong answer

Here is an extract from student response to this question, with the examiner's annotations and final comments. It receives high marks.

Dickens shows how Tiny Tim's family are unable to save his life without medical or financial aid – a comment on social inequality. **1** *Through the choice of the diminutive 'Tiny Tim' and the references to his 'little stool' and 'withered little hand', Dickens highlights the child's disability.* **2** *Tim's likely death is suggested when the Spirit envisages the child's absence, by citing 'a vacant seat' and 'a crutch without an owner'.* **3** *The phrase, 'carefully preserved', reveals the profound loss that will be felt by Tim's grieving family.* **4** *Scrooge's surprising outburst, 'Oh, no, [...] say he will be spared.' earns him some sympathy from the reader, but a rebuke from the Spirit and a reminder of his previous callous thought about the poor.* **5** *Not content with Scrooge's 'penitence', the Spirit mocks his arrogance in believing that he is in a position to decide 'what men shall live, what men shall die'.* **6** *The Spirit compares Scrooge to an 'Insect on the leaf pronouncing on [...] his hungry brothers in the dust!'. Dickens uses this metaphor to expose the hypocrisy of the rich, who condemn the poor from their position of comfort, acquired only by their accumulation of wealth.* **7** *In a display of Dickensian irony, it is at this point that Bob proposes a toast to Scrooge describing him as 'the Founder of the feast'.* **8**

1 Immediate focus on the question and the significance of the passage in relation to the theme of the question

2 Good attention to Dickens' choice of vocabulary and its intended effect

3 Sophisticated observation about the way the Spirit suggests Tiny Tim's death

4 Sensitive analysis of the impact of the phrase 'carefully preserved'

5 Good use of quotation

6 Confident commentary on the Spirit's response to Scrooge

7 A good section that includes explicit reference to the question and to one of Dickens' methods

8 Useful reference to Dickens' use of irony

Examiner's comments

This response is critical, exploratory, and well-structured. The appropriate choice of examples supports a sensitive reading of Dickens' approach to social inequality as presented in the printed extract. Subject terminology is used accurately and there is evidence of insightful analysis.

Retrieval

Answer the questions below. Cover the answers column with a piece of paper and write down as many answers as you can. Check and repeat.

	Questions	Answers
1	What is Scrooge's attitude towards the poor at the beginning of the novel?	Indifference
2	Complete the quotation: '"If these ________ remain unaltered by the ______ the child will die"'	'"If these shadows remain unaltered by the Future the child will die"'
3	What point about poverty is the narrator making, in Stave I, when he describes the 'ragged men and boys' gathering around the great fire in a brazier in the street?	They are warming themselves on a freezing night in their ragged clothes, by getting close to 'free' warmth as no other option is available to them
4	Who acts as a mouthpiece for Dickens' concern for the poor?	The 'portly gentlemen'
5	Complete the quotation: '"we should make some slight ________ for the Poor and ________"'	'"we should make some slight provision for the Poor and destitute"'
6	How many rooms are there in the house that the Cratchit family live in?	Four
7	What do the two wretched children, hidden beneath the robes the Ghost of Christmas, represent?	The Girl represents 'Want', the Boy represents 'Ignorance'
8	Who considers Fred to be 'poor enough'?	Scrooge
9	How does Scrooge feel when he sees the 'surplus population' in close-up at the Cratchits?	Ashamed

Put paper here

Previous questions

Now go back and use these questions to check your knowledge of previous topics.

	Questions	Answers
1	Name two things Dickens uses to chart Scrooge's progress.	Two from: light / dark / warmth / cold
2	Which two characters act as models for Scrooge's redemption?	Bob; Fred
3	Which of the three Ghosts of Christmas tells Scrooge that their business with him is his 'reclamation'?	The Ghost of Christmas Past

Put paper here

Now turn to page 121 and complete Practice question 16.

16 Family

How family is presented

Plot

The novel opens, more or less immediately, with Scrooge refusing an invitation from his nephew, Fred, to Christmas dinner with Fred and his family, despite Fred's repeated appeal:

'"I want nothing from you; I ask nothing of you; why cannot we be friends?"

Later, Scrooge observes himself as a young boy, apparently rejected by his own father and excluded from family time at Christmas. He also sees how close he was to his little sister, Fan:

'"Good afternoon," said Scrooge.' 'a little girl [...] came darting in, and putting her arms about his neck, and often kissing him, addressed him as her "Dear, dear brother."'

Later still, Scrooge's sees his former fiancée, Belle, surrounded by her happy family. Scrooge reflects on the fact that he might have had such a family and such a daughter; he bitterly regrets having let Belle go.

In the end, Scrooge takes up Fred's invitation, having been taught the value of family ties through the Spirits. At Fred's, Scrooge feels:

'... at home in five minutes. Nothing could be heartier.'

Direct address

The narrator comments directly on the theme of family in Stave III telling us, of the Cratchits:

'They were not a handsome family; [...] But they were happy, grateful, pleased with one another, and contented'

Of Fred's family, the narrator comments:

'they were a musical family, and knew what they were about'

Characters acting as mouthpieces

Both Fred and Bob act as mouthpieces for the author in praise of family life. Fred proposes a toast to his Uncle, despite his bad temper, because he *is* his uncle and he wishes in his heart that he has:

'"A Merry Christmas and a Happy New Year [...] whatever he is!"'

Bob, in a far more sombre scene, speaks of the strength of family ties, reminding his family that:

'"however and whenever we part from one another, I am sure we shall none of us forget poor Tiny Tim—shall we—or this first parting that there was among us?"'

Knowledge THEMES

16 Family

Characters representing family

All the families represent the theme of family. Whether in high spirits at Christmas in Stave III or mourning the 'death' of Tiny Tim in Stave IV, the Cratchit family show their mutual love, respect, and compassion; supporting one another through good times and bad:

Bob: '"A Merry Christmas to us all, my dears. God bless us!" Which all the family re-echoed.'

Another poor family represents this theme in Stave IV, when news of Scrooge's death lightens the hearts of Caroline, her husband and her children; making their home 'happier' because they are able to put off paying their debt for a little longer.

'Mrs. Cratchit kissed him, his daughters kissed him, the two young Cratchits kissed him, and Peter and himself shook hands.'

REVISION TIP

Some commentators believe that by revealing aspects of Scrooge's lonely childhood and fractured family relationships Dickens may be suggesting that this contributed to Scrooge's isolation in later years.

REMEMBER

There is a turning point in the story when Scrooge sees the happiness shared by the Fezziwig family. When the Ghost of Christmas Past plays down Fezziwig's benevolence, Scrooge becomes 'heated' and heartily defends him.

Five key points about family

1. Scrooge is introduced as a solitary character, indifferent to family and with no friends.
2. The Spirits show Scrooge happy families, revealing what he has denied himself through his rejection of kindness and human connection.
3. Scrooge's recognition of the happiness of the Fezziwig family is a turning point in the story.
4. The sheer family joy expressed by the Cratchits at Christmas touches Scrooge's humanity and shows him that a loving family will support each other despite facing hardship and grief.
5. Scrooge joins Fred on Christmas Day, restoring family ties; completing the 'arc' of the story.

REVISION TIP

Make a list of Scrooge's relatives who are mentioned in the novel. Write a sentence or two about how each one contributes to his fictional 'life' and journey through the novel.

Writing about family

Sample answer 1: not a strong answer

Here is an extract from a student response to this question, with the examiner's annotations and final comments. It receives less than half marks.

Extracts from Stave I, from: '"Why, where's our Martha?" cried Bob Cratchit, looking round.' to: 'Tiny Tim, excited by the two young Cratchits, beat on the table with the handle of his knife, and feebly cried Hurrah!'

> Starting with this extract, explore how Dickens presents the theme of family in *A Christmas Carol*.
>
> **[30 marks]**

In this extract, Dickens presents the Cratchit family on Christmas Day. Unknown to them, they are being watched by Scrooge and the Ghost of Christmas Present. **1** *The Ghost has brought Scrooge to see the Cratchit family, firstly, to show him the love and respect paid to Bob Cratchit, who Scrooge treats very badly, when he is at home among his loving family.* **2** *Secondly, to show Scrooge what happiness is brought to families at Christmas. Thirdly, to show Scrooge how cruel it is that Tiny Tim will die without medical care.* **3** *Fourthly, to remind Scrooge how poor people make the best of things at Christmas for the sake of the children.* **4** *In the paragraph that begins with 'Such a bustle ensued'* **5** *Dickens shows how the Cratchit family work together to make the best Christmas they can have. Everyone has a job to do and they do it without complaining.* **6** *They all live together without any fights and are a model family.* **7**

1. This could be developed.
2. This could be made into a valid point about the work/home persona of Bob but it needs to be developed to achieve this.
3. The point about Tiny Tim might also be credit-worthy, if developed.
4. Dickens' methods should be identified and analysed here, although the purposes suggested are potentially relevant and useful.
5. This is the only close reference to the text.
6. This is correct, but no analysis of Dickens' method or purpose is offered.
7. This point lacks development or analysis.

Examiner's comments

This is a largely narrative response which does not go much beyond identifying the characters in the Cratchit family. The point regarding the Spirit's purpose in showing Scrooge the Cratchit family's home life, is the strongest part of the answer as it hints at Dickens' wider purpose, but this is not developed.

16 Family

Sample answer 2: a strong answer

Here is an extract from a student response to the question on page 71, with the examiner's annotations and final comments. It receives high marks.

Dickens presents the theme of family through his sympathetic portrayal of the Cratchits, using description and quotation. ❶ Bob is playful with his little son as he 'gallops' home from church with Tim on his back, like a 'blood horse [...] rampant'. ❷ Bob's 'high spirits' decline when told Martha is 'Not coming'. Hearing her father's bewildered 'Not coming upon Christmas Day!' and seeing him so downcast, Martha 'ran into his arms' showing the deep affection between Bob and his children. ❸ All the children contribute to preparing the dinner in an energetic and joyous way, shown through Dickens' use of a sequence of 'active' verbs ❹: Peter 'mashed' the potatoes, Martha 'dusted' the plates; it suggests a picture of harmonious industry. ❺ Dickens emphasises the family's admiration for Tiny Tim's acceptance of his disability, as Bob recounts how Tim hoped that he might remind others of Jesus' miracles. Dickens is perhaps reminding Scrooge, and us, that miracles are unlikely to help Tiny Tim, and active intervention is needed. ❻ Bob's voice 'trembled more when he said that Tiny Tim was growing strong and hearty'. Hearing Bob's emotion is a powerful way of eliciting sympathy and Dickens enhances this by concluding with Tiny Tim's own 'feeble' cry of 'Hurrah!'. ❼

❶ Two methods of presenting the theme are identified.

❷ Useful quotation to show Bob's playfulness

❸ Concise way of showing the family's love for one another

❹ Useful identification of Dickens' method

❺ Well-expressed appreciation of the effect created through the active verbs

❻ Useful analysis of Dickens' purpose here and a sensitive response to it

❼ Good point about the power of the 'heard' voice

Examiner's comments

While this part of the answer does not go beyond the extract, the analysis is secure and comments are thoughtful and generally analytical. This shows a clear understanding of Dickens' language choices and purpose.

Retrieval

Answer the questions below. Cover the answers column with a piece of paper and write down as many as you can. Check and repeat.

	Questions	Answers
1	What relation is Fred to Scrooge?	Scrooge's nephew
2	Complete the quotation: '"I want ______ from you; I ask nothing of you; why cannot we be ______?"'	'"I want <u>nothing</u> from you; I ask nothing of you; why cannot we be <u>friends</u>?"'
3	What childhood experience may have contributed to Scrooge's isolation in later years?	Being excluded from the family at Christmas by his father
4	What does Scrooge feel when the Ghost of Christmas Past shows him Belle and her family?	Regret at letting Belle go
5	Complete the quotation: 'They were not a ________ family; but they were happy, _______, pleased with one another, and _________.	'They were not a <u>handsome</u> family; but they were happy, <u>grateful</u>, pleased with one another, and <u>contented</u>.
6	Which of the families presented in the novel is described as 'musical'?	Fred's family
7	Which characters act as Dickens' mouthpieces for his views about family?	Fred; Bob
8	Complete the quotation: '"I am sure we shall none of us forget ____ ____ ___—shall we—or this first parting that there was among us?"'	'"I am sure we shall none of us forget <u>poor Tiny Tim</u>—shall we—or this first parting that there was among us?"'
9	What qualities do the Cratchit family show to one another in good times and bad?	Mutual love, respect, and compassion; supporting one another through good times and bad
10	What makes the home of Caroline and her husband 'happier'?	News of Scrooge's death

Put paper here

Previous questions

Now go back and use these questions to check your knowledge of previous topics.

	Questions	Answers
1	What is Scrooge's attitude towards the poor at the beginning of the novel?	Indifference
2	Who acts as a mouthpiece for Dickens' concern for the poor?	The 'portly gentlemen'

Put paper here

Now turn to page 117 and complete Practice question 13.

17 Time

How time is presented

A Christmas Carol appears to begin in the author's 'present', gradually we learn that the story takes place in an indefinite time, in the past. The title indicates that the story is set at Christmas and Scrooge's past Christmases are used to highlight his evolving character and experiences through time.

A Christmas Carol is not about 'time travel', however the Spirits transport Scrooge through time. Time is the medium that Dickens uses to reflect upon what Scrooge was like in his youth, what he became in his middle years, and how he was redeemed.

Plot

The plot is revealed in three distinct time frames – Staves I, III and V are set in the present. In Stave III Scrooge is an invisible observer of the present, whereas in Staves I and V he is an active participant in it.

From Stave II: 'the Ghost [...] saying as it did so, "Let us see another Christmas!"

Stave II takes place in the past, but time does not stand still in this stave, instead jumping from vison to vision.

Stave IV is the most unsettling for Scrooge. Set in the future, again the visions don't appear chronologically.

'Scrooge's former self grew larger at the words, and the room became a little darker and more dirty. [...] but how all this was brought about, Scrooge knew no more than you do.'

The timeframe shows us that while Scrooge's present was shaped by his past, the future will be shaped by the actions (and inaction) of the present-day Scrooge, unless he changes his ways.

Direct address

The narrator addresses the reader directly in the opening stave to tell us that Marley's name stood 'years afterward' above the warehouse door. The narrator also consciously sets the story in the unidentified past, using the fairy-tale introduction:

'Once upon a time—of all the good days in the year, on Christmas Eve'

Characters discussing time

Dickens uses the three Spirits to act as mouthpieces for his views (despite the Spirit of Christmas Yet to Come's silence) in each of the timeframes – past, present, and future.

In Stave IV Scrooge speculates to the Ghost of Christmas Yet to Come:

'"You are about to show me shadows of the things that have not happened, but will happen in the time before us"'

The primary function of the Spirits is to show Scrooge what he was in times past, what he is 'today', and what he might be in the future.

Characters representing time

The Spirits each represent the theme of time through their roles as Past, Present, and Yet to Come.

Repeated motifs, symbols, and images

All three of the Christmas Spirits are symbolic.

Motifs associated with the theme of time may be found throughout in the chimes of clocks and bells.

Marley's Ghost is quite particular about when each of the Spirits will visit Scrooge:

'"Expect the first to-morrow when the bell tolls One. […] the second on the next night at the same hour. […] The third, upon the next night when the last stroke of Twelve has ceased to vibrate."'

REVISION TIP

Make a list of the ways in which Dickens reminds the reader of time passing in each stave.

Five key points about time

1. Time is the medium for the plot, covering Scrooge's past, present, and future.
2. Marley's Ghost reveals another 'dimension' – 'eternity'.
3. Time is manipulated and distorted by the Spirits, and Scrooge is confused and disorientated by this.
4. Clocks, watches chimes, bells, light, and darkness are used to show time passing, reminding Scrooge (and the reader) of mortality.
5. The Spirits remind Scrooge that his time for change is limited – if Scrooge wants to change his future, he must change his behaviour now while he is still alive.

Knowledge THEMES

17 Time

Writing about time

Sample answer 1: not a strong answer

Here is an extract from a student response to this question, with the examiner's annotations and final comments. It receives less than half marks.

Extract from Stave IV, from: 'The Ghost of Christmas Yet To Come conveyed him, as before—though at a different time, he thought' to: '"Oh, tell me I may sponge away the writing on this stone!"'

> Starting with this extract, explore how Dickens presents the theme of time in *A Christmas Carol*.
>
> **[30 marks]**

This extract is taken from the end of the novel when Scrooge persuades the Ghost to let him live to be a better man. ❶ The Ghost is sneaky with Scrooge because when he asks to be shown 'what I shall be in days to come' he shows him his grave, which is not what Scrooge expected, although everyone does end up dead, so the Ghost is not being dishonest. ❷ Scrooge is afraid that the visions he has been shown by Ghost of Christmas Yet to Come apply directly to him, so that he will be spoken of carelessly when he dies, and he will be robbed as he lies on his deathbed, and he will end up in an overgrown graveyard with nothing on his headstone except for a name. ❸ Time is the theme that concerns Scrooge here, as he realises that both now and in the past he has been a bad employer, making Bob work in the cold and paying him a pittance, a bad fiancé of Belle turning from her love to love money more, and a bad friend to Marley, working on the day of his funeral. ❹ As Scrooge becomes more upset by the thought of death, he begs the Spirit to reassure him that he may, in time, change his ways. ❺ By promising to 'change' Scrooge shows that he intends to put the past and his present, miserly ways behind him, and become a new man in the future, showing the importance of time in this novel. ❻

❶ Identifies Scrooge's intention to become a better man.

❷ This is not a persuasive argument. 'Sneaky' is too casual a word to use in an exam answer.

❸ This is better attention to the text and to Scrooge's worries at this point in the novel.

❹ Some understanding is shown but the theme of time is becoming a little lost.

❺ This is an accurate observation.

❻ There is an attempt to sum up Scrooge's new resolution in relation to the theme of time but this has not been developed.

Examiner's comments

The answer is relevant, and there is a little explanation of what Scrooge feels about the future. However, while acknowledging that time is an important theme in the passage, the response lacks any kind of detail about how Dickens presents the theme of time.

Sample answer 2: a strong answer

Here is an extract from a student response to this question, with the examiner's annotations and final comments. It receives high marks.

The word 'time' appears in 'A Christmas Carol' over 80 times and it is the most frequently used noun in the novel. ❶ *Dickens draws attention to the theme of 'time', in this extract, by revealing how Scrooge becomes conscious of the Spirit's ability to manipulate it: 'there seemed no order in these latter visions, save that they were in the Future'.* ❷ *The 'time-scale' of Scrooge's experiences appears to be distorted. Dickens uses a capital letter for 'Future', emphasising its importance as the 'dimension' Scrooge finds himself in.* ❸ *As he does elsewhere in the novel, Dickens has subtly shifted into telling the tale from Scrooge's perspective, showing us Scrooge's perception of the movement of time.* ❹ *Scrooge notes that the Spirit now seems to be in a 'hurry', 'the Spirit did not stay for anything, but went straight on' which suggests the pressure of time experienced by the Ghost, causing Scrooge to ask it to 'tarry for a moment'. The contrast of the verbs 'hurry' and 'tarry' emphasises the opposite desires of the Spirit and Scrooge.* ❺ *Scrooge expresses his wish to 'behold what I shall be, in days to come' using the future tense in a positive way, showing his anticipation of a new way of life.* ❻ *As the Spirit continues to point away from Scrooge's office, Scrooge detaches himself from the Spirit to satisfy*

Continued

❶ Clear focus on the theme of time in the novel as a whole. The candidate explores the wider novel in a later part of the complete response.

❷ The point about the manipulation of time is relevant here.

❸ Clear language comment about Dickens' capitalisation of the word 'Future'

❹ This is a subtle language point about the shift in perspective on the movement of time.

❺ Well-focused on time-associated vocabulary such as 'hurry' and 'tarry'

❻ Another sensitive observation about Scrooge's positive attitude linked to his future

Knowledge THEMES

17 Time

his curiosity, but is disappointed not to have seen his 'future self'. 7 Scrooge confronts the outcome of his previous, selfish existence when he is shown the headstone in a graveyard 'overrun by grass and weeds'; both aspects relate to the theme of time. A headstone – with no meaningful inscription beyond Scrooge's name connotes the permanence of 'death'. The idea of a neglected 'wilderness' growing around it suggests an untended grave; a pointless 'memorial' of a wasted life. The repetition of the sardonic comment 'worthy!' perhaps suggests a flash of self-knowledge. 8 Scrooge begs the Spirit to accept that he is no longer 'the man I was' and to allow him time to adopt 'an altered life'. Dickens pulls together the past and the future in these phrases highlighting the theme of time. 9 Scrooge promises to do the impossible: 'I will live in the Past, the Present and the Future', with each dimension capitalised for emphasis. This seems to secure the Spirit's sympathy, at last. 10 While many ordinary 'sinners' long to be able to wipe out their past, Dickens puts an interesting twist on this concept for Scrooge, who, in longing to 'sponge away the writing on this stone!' seeks to erase his potential future. His wish releases him from his 'time travel' and back into his own bed. 11

7 Understanding of Scrooge's feelings, linked to his future, but a slightly narrative feel to this point

8 This point is very clearly analysed in relation to the theme of time.

9 This is quite a sophisticated reading of one of Dickens' methods.

10 The student offers an interesting observation on Scrooge's intention to live in all times, at once.

11 This is a considered conclusion to a thoughtful response.

Examiner's comments

The student offers a critical exploration of Dickens' treatment of the theme of time in the given extract. There is a sense of a developing argument which is well-supported from the text. The response is clearly expressed and focused on the task throughout, with some effective analysis of Dickens' use of language.

Retrieval

Answer the questions below. Cover the answers column with a piece of paper and write down as many as you can. Check and repeat.

	Questions	Answers
1	What kind of stories tend to begin with 'Once upon a time'?	Fairy tales
2	Is *A Christmas Carol* about time travel?	No – time is the medium for exploring Scrooge's character at different times in his life
3	Which of the staves are set in the present?	Stave I; Stave III; Stave V
4	What is the significance of Scrooge being shown a selection of his past Christmases?	They highlight his evolving character and experiences through time
5	Complete the quotation: 'Scrooge's former self grew _____ at the words, and the room became a little darker and _____ _____.'	'Scrooge's former self grew <u>larger</u> at the words, and the room became a little darker and <u>more</u> <u>dirty</u>.'
6	Whose name does the narrator say stood 'years afterward' above the warehouse door?	Marley's
7	What is the primary function of the Spirits?	To show Scrooge what he was in times past, what he is 'today', and what he might be in the future
8	What motifs are associated with the theme of time?	Chimes of clocks; bells
9	Complete the quotation: '"Expect the first tomorrow when the ____ ____ ____ [...] the second on the next night at the same hour [...] The third, upon the next night when the last stroke of Twelve has ceased __ _______."'	'"Expect the first to-morrow when the <u>bell</u> <u>tolls</u> <u>One</u> [...] the second on the next night at the same hour [...] The third, upon the next night when the last stroke of Twelve has ceased <u>to</u> <u>vibrate</u>."'

Put paper here

Previous questions

Now go back and use these questions to check your knowledge of previous topics.

	Questions	Answers
1	What does Scrooge feel when the Ghost of Christmas Past shows him Belle and her family?	Regret at letting Belle go
2	Which characters act as Dickens' mouthpieces for his views about family?	Fred; Bob

Put paper here

Now turn to page 110 and complete Practice question 8.

Knowledge THEMES

18 Christmas spirit

How Christmas spirit is presented

Christmas spirit is associated with themes of good will, charity, benevolence, and family celebrations.

The religious significance of Christmas is largely only implied in *A Christmas Carol*, otherwise, Christmas is presented as a festival bringing families together physically or through fond thoughts.

Plot

The Christmas spirit is a dominant theme throughout the plot, which charts Scrooge's shift in attitude away from 'Bah!', 'Humbug!' to his 'reclaimed' self at the end, when:

'it was always said […] that he knew how to keep Christmas well, if any man alive possessed the knowledge.'

Direct address

The narrator tells us directly, in Stave III, something about the Christmas spirit and how it can make people behave and feel:

'it is good to be children sometimes, and never better than at Christmas, when its mighty Founder was a child himself.'

Characters discussing Christmas spirit

Fred and Scrooge have a discussion, of sorts, about the value of Christmas, in Stave I. Fred is also the most vocal of the characters who act as the author's mouthpiece on the theme of the Christmas spirit, showing his appreciation of Christmas as:

'"a good time; a kind, forgiving, charitable, pleasant time"'

The portly gentlemen also attempt to convince Scrooge of the importance of charity at Christmas time:

'"At this festive season of the year […] it is more than usually desirable that we should make some slight provision for the poor and destitute."'

Characters representing the Christmas spirit

The Ghost of Christmas Present represents the theme of Christmas spirit. His appearance, seated on a 'throne' of festive food, is described as that of:

'a jolly Giant, glorious to see; who bore a glowing torch […] and held it up, high up, to shed its light on Scrooge […] and on its head […] a holly wreath, set here and there with shining icicles'.

The Ghost introduces himself as one of a long line of Christmases spanning all the generations since the birth of Christ.

Repeated motifs, symbols, and images

The theme of Christmas spirit is supported by a range of motifs usually associated with warmth, light, and brightness.

At Fezziwig's party:

'the lamps were trimmed, fuel was heaped upon the fire; and the warehouse was as snug, and warm, and dry, and bright a ball-room, as you would desire to see upon a winter's night.'

At the miner's hut:

'A light shone from the window [...] they found a cheerful company assembled round a glowing fire'

REMEMBER

Dickens wrote at a time when Christianity was the main religion practised in Britain.

Five key points about Christmas spirit

1. The theme of Christmas is integral, and provides the framework for the story.
2. Each of the Spirits presents a Christmas 'time'; in the past, present, or the future.
3. 'Christmas' is presented as 'a state of mind' as much as it is a time of year.
4. It is associated with themes of good will, charity, and benevolence, as well as the birth of Christ.
5. Dickens suggests the Christmas spirit should be honoured every day.

REVISION TIP

Make a list of each time the celebration of Christmas Day occurs in the novel – compile a list of words that Dickens uses on each occasion to show the reader why Christmas is such a special time of year.

Knowledge THEMES

18 Christmas spirit

Writing about Christmas spirit

Sample answer 1: not a strong answer

Here is an extract from a student response to this question, with the examiner's annotations and final comments. It receives less than half marks.

Extract from Stave I, from: '"What place is this?" asked Scrooge.' to: '...and had remembered those he cared for at a distance, and had known that they delighted to remember him.'

> Starting with this extract, explore how Dickens presents the theme of the Christmas spirit in *A Christmas Carol*.
>
> **[30 marks]**

The Ghost of Christmas Present makes Scrooge realise what Christmas means to families. ❶ Scrooge is amazed to see another poor family having a merry time at Christmas. Whole families are crammed together in their 'holiday attire' which reminds us of Mrs Cratchit with ribbons on her dress. ❷ Scrooge discovers that the family are miners who 'labour in the bowels of the earth' where there is no light, but in the hut there is light shining to show the Christmas cheer. ❸ Next the Ghost of Christmas Past takes Scrooge to a lighthouse. Dickens describes it as a solitary place which makes me think of Scrooge in Stave I where he is described as 'solitary as an oyster'. ❹ The lighthouse men have lit a fire and have grog to celebrate Christmas. Dickens makes the men seem quite rough with 'horny hands', but they still think of Christmas as a good time like Fred said in Stave I. ❺ The Ghost wants Scrooge to realise that all different types of people 'keep' Christmas and that he should, too. ❻

❶ This is a focused point.

❷ This is a well-observed comparison.

❸ This point about light is a good one but could have been developed.

❹ The student is showing some knowledge of the text but is not maintaining a consistent focus on the question asked.

❺ This attempts to analyse the effect that Dickens is creating but it needs further development. The link to Fred's speech about Christmas is appropriate.

❻ This is a fair summary of the Ghost's purpose in taking Scrooge to these different places.

Examiner's comments

In this answer, there are some creditworthy points about the 'keeping' of Christmas and a comment about Dickens' purpose but these need to be developed.

Sample answer 2: a strong answer

Here is an extract from a student response to this question, with the examiner's annotations and final comments. It receives high marks.

Dickens uses this passage to emphasise the universal importance of Christmas spirit. He does this through presenting ordinary people whose lives are brightened, literally and figuratively, by celebrating Christmas. (1) Dickens offers reminders of a festival that brings people 'good or bad' together. This coming-together, both physically – 'Joining their horny hands over the rough table' or mentally – 'remembered those he cared for at a distance', represents the essence of the meaning of Christmas. (2) The mining family and the lighthouse keepers are depicted bathed in light and warmth. Dickens frequently uses such images to symbolise comfort, contentedness, enlightenment; here light symbolises the spirit of Christmas shining bright. (3) The miner's cottage has light in the window, and a 'glowing fire'. In the lighthouse, the men had 'made a fire' which 'shed out a ray of brightness on the awful sea'. (4) In all locations, there is song – one of Dickens' motifs for human goodness. (5) The old man in the miner's cottage was 'singing them a Christmas song', the elder lighthouse keeper 'struck up a sturdy song'. Even at sea, with no light or fire described, 'every man among them hummed a Christmas tune, or had a Christmas thought, or spoke [...] of some by-gone Christmas Day'. (6) Dickens is showing us how the Christmas spirit touches all who 'honour' the day, and how, as Fred might say, it does them 'good'. (7)

(1) Good focus on Dickens' purpose and brief reference is made to Dickens' methods in the passage

(2) Use of quotation is helpful, well-explained and focused on the question

(3) The student recognises one of Dickens' methods and its purpose here and places that in the context of the whole novel.

(4) Good choice of supporting text

(5) Useful reference to a recurring image

(6) The idea about song is comprehensively supported from the passage.

(7) Neat ending, quoting Fred to endorse the student's conclusion about Dickens' presentation of the Christmas spirit

Examiner's comments

Focused almost exclusively on the passage, there is very good use of the text to illustrate Dickens' methods and purposeful comments on Dickens' allusions to song.

Retrieval

Answer the questions below. Cover the answers column with a piece of paper and write down as many as you can. Check and repeat.

	Questions	Answers
1	Name two other themes associated with Christmas spirit.	Two from: charity / benevolence / family celebrations / good will
2	Which two words does Scrooge use to Fred in Stave I, to express his initial disgust about Christmas?	'"Bah!"'; "Humbug!"'
3	Complete the quotation: 'it is good __ __ ______ sometimes, and never better than at Christmas, when its ______ ______ was a child himself.'	'it is good to be children sometimes, and never better than at Christmas, when its mighty Founder was a child himself.'
4	Who acts as the main mouthpiece for Dickens on the theme of Christmas?	Fred
5	Complete the quotation: '"a good time; a kind, ______, ______ pleasant time"'.	'"a good time; a kind, forgiving, charitable pleasant time"'.
6	Which of the ghosts is described as wearing 'a holly wreath' on his head, and carrying 'a glowing torch'?	The Ghost of Christmas Present
7	Name two motifs that are associated with Christmas spirit.	Two from: warmth / light / brightness
8	Complete the quotation: 'the lamps were trimmed, fuel was heaped upon the fire; and the warehouse was __ ____, ___ ____, ___ ___, and bright a ball-room as you would desire to see upon a ______' ____.'	'the lamps were trimmed, fuel was heaped upon the fire; and the warehouse was as snug, and warm, and dry, and bright a ball-room as you would desire to see upon a winter's' night.'
9	Whose Christmas party does the quotation in question 8 refer to?	Fezziwig's

Previous questions

Use the questions below to check your knowledge from previous chapters.

	Questions	Answers
1	Which of the staves are set in the present?	Stave I; Stave III; Stave V
2	What motifs are associated with the theme of time?	Chimes of clocks; bells
3	Whose name does the narrator say stood 'years afterward' above the warehouse door?	Marley's

Now turn to page 112 and complete Practice question 9.

19 Wealth, greed, and charity

How wealth, greed, and charity are presented

Plot

Dickens shows how a man like Scrooge, whose life is devoted to making money, but not spending it, may be converted to a benevolent friend and employer, and a willing donor to charity.

On giving money to the 'portly gentlemen' after his redemption, Scrooge says:

'"Not a farthing less. A great many back-payments are included in it, I assure you."'

Direct address

The narrator comments directly on Scrooge's avarice in the description of Scrooge in Stave I. He also tells us directly at the end of the story how Scrooge has changed, fulfilling his promises to Bob and much more.

'"I'll raise your salary, and endeavour to assist your struggling family" […] Scrooge was better than his word. He did it all, and infinitely more'.

Characters discussing wealth, greed, and charity

Various characters act as a mouthpiece for Dicken's views on wealth and greed. Each speaks of the life-sapping quality of pursuing money for money's sake. Fred is very clear on the matter:

'"His wealth is of no use to him. He don't do any good with it. He don't make himself comfortable with it."'

Marley's Ghost is very clear in his message that his love of money has resulted in his miserable afterlife:

'"… in life my spirit never roved beyond the narrow limits of our money-changing hole; and weary journeys lie before me!"'

Belle tells her fiancé, Scrooge – as a young man:

'"I have seen your nobler aspirations fall off one by one, until the master-passion, Gain, engrosses you."'

The Ghost of Christmas Past provokes Scrooge by observing of Fezziwig:

'"He has spent but a few pounds of your mortal money […] Is that so much that he deserves this praise?"'

The unpleasant businessmen who are introduced by the Ghost of Christmas Yet to Come specifically discuss Scrooge's money:

'"What has he done with his money?" […] "I haven't heard," said the man" […] yawning again. […] "He hasn't left it to *me*. That's all I know."'

Scrooge's debtors, Caroline and her husband, also discuss money:

'"To whom will our debt be transferred?" "I don't know. But, before that time, we shall be ready with the money […] it would be a bad fortune indeed to find so merciless a creditor in his successor."'

Knowledge THEMES

19 Wealth, greed, and charity

Characters representing greed, wealth, and charity

Scrooge most frequently represents the theme of wealth and greed.

Greed is also seen in the businessmen that Scrooge sees in Stave IV, who: 'chinked the money in their pockets […] and trifled thoughtfully with their great gold seals;'

We also see characters who have wealth but who represent charity, such as the 'portly gentlemen'.

Repeated motifs, symbols, and images

Greed is presented through figurative language, including descriptions of Scrooge's nature:

'Oh! But he was a tight-fisted hand at the grindstone, Scrooge! a squeezing, wrenching, grasping, scraping, clutching, covetous, old sinner!'

And through the appearance of some of the wealthy businessmen:

'a great fat man with a monstrous chin'

'red-faced gentleman with a pendulous excrescence on the end of his nose, that shook like the gills of a turkey-cock'

REVISION TIP

The vivid descriptions of the wealthy businessmen make the reader associate the pursuit of money with physical ugliness.

REMEMBER

Wealth, greed, and charity are seen as themes related to or contrasted with poverty, the poor, and social injustice.

Five key points about wealth, greed, and charity

1. Dickens shows that Scrooge's greed has led to him becoming isolated and cruel at the start of the story.
2. Characters are defined by their attitudes towards money, reflected in their appearance.
3. Dickens promotes the idea that money should be used sensibly, shared, and given to charity.
4. Scrooge's redemption is shown through his transformation from a miserly, greedy man to one who is generous and helps others.
5. Dickens condemns greed and hoarding of wealth, conveying the idea that happiness and joy comes from generosity and helping others, not from money.

REVISION TIP

Find an example from the novel for each of these five key points about wealth, greed, and charity.

Sample answers

Sample answer 1: not a strong answer

Here is an extract from a student response to this question, with the examiner's annotations and final comments. It receives less than half marks.

Extract from Stave IV from: '"And now undo *my* bundle, Joe," said the first woman…' to: '"He frightened every one away from him when he was alive, to profit us when he was dead! Ha, ha, ha!"'

> Starting with this extract, explore how Dickens presents the theme of greed in *A Christmas Carol*.
>
> **[30 marks]**

In this extract, Dickens presents three very greedy people: Old Joe, Mrs Dilber, and the charwoman. ❶ *Old Joe runs a horrible shop and pays for any old rubbish, including 'rusty keys', 'old rags, bottles', and 'bones', but Joe is greedy and does not give a very good price.* ❷ *Although the women are poor, they are thieves (unlike Mrs Cratchit who is poor but honest) and Dickens, in this section, is showing us that Mrs Dilber and the charwoman are disgustingly greedy.* ❸ *Mrs Dilber has just shown her stolen goods, when the charwoman wants her turn. She has pulled down the bed curtains from Scrooge's bed while his body was on it. This is not only creepy but shows the lengths that the charwoman is prepared to go to for the sake of her greed.* ❹ *She then tells Joe and the other thieves, quite proudly, that she saved the best shirt from being 'wasted' by taking it off the corpse herself, to get a good price.* ❺ *Even Joe, who knowingly 'fences' stolen goods, is shocked by the charwoman's outrageous greed.* ❻

❶ Immediate focus on the question's focus of greed

❷ This is factually correct and includes a reference to Joe's greed.

❸ The student compares the two thieves with Mrs Cratchit; all three are poor but only Mrs Cratchit is 'honest'; it is a reasonable point but it is not developed.

❹ Takes a while to get to a relevant point about greed

❺ Good point but not fully explored

❻ This is better, as there is some sense of the lengths that the charwoman has gone to, to 'get a good price'.

Examiner's comments

There is some explanation of Dickens' presentation of 'greed' here. The term is used in each of the short paragraphs and text from the passage is used to support points made. The points made would benefit from further development.

EXAM TIP

Always try to develop the points that you are making when analysing text. You need to go beyond quoting relevant text; you must comment clearly on its significance.

Knowledge THEMES

19 Wealth, greed, and charity

Sample answer 2: a strong answer

Here is an extract from a student response to the question on page 87, with the examiner's annotations and final comments. It receives high marks.

In the characters of the laundress and the charwoman, Dickens presents 'greed' personified. Old Joe also has a symbolic role, representing 'commerce' in its basest form, by greedily profiting from the crimes of others. **1** *Dickens allows us to hear how the charwoman takes pride in her theft and is defiant when challenged: replying 'cooly': 'I certainly shan't hold my hand, when I can get anything in it by reaching it out'. Dickens' use of the noun 'hand' and the verb 'reaching' help to underline the grasping attitude of the charwoman, underscoring her greed.* **2** *More shocking still is the charwoman's brazen admission that she literally stole the shirt off Scrooge's back.* **3** *She boasts it was a 'waste' to have Scrooge buried in his 'best' shirt. She literally 'adds insult to injury' by suggesting that Scrooge 'can't look uglier',* **4** *in the calico shirt that she swapped for his best one. Dickens amplifies the effect by the presence of Scrooge, silently observing while not knowing the identity of the corpse that they have robbed.* **5** *Dickens tells us his 'disgust [...] could hardly have been greater, though they had been obscene demons, marketing the corpse itself' – creating a powerful image of the 'diabolical' thieves.* **6** *The charwoman mocks Scrooge for having 'frightened every one away from him when he was alive, to profit us when he was dead!' which emphasises the greed and opportunism of the thieves.* **7** *Finally, Dickens' allows the laundress's unfeeling laughter to ring in the reader's ears to amplify his message about the ugliness of greed.* **8**

1 The student identifies personification and symbolism as two of Dickens' presentational methods.

2 Dickens allows us to hear the charwoman's boast and there is useful analysis of vocabulary.

3 This is quite a neat point, playing on a familiar colloquialism.

4 This is extended at the end of the paragraph by alluding to the saying 'to add insult to injury'.

5 The presence of Scrooge is another method, usefully identified.

6 Dickens' use of this extended simile is noted as another method.

7 This is a good point linking greed with another vicious quality.

8 An apt comment on the final line of the passage and its impact in underlining the greed of the thieves

Examiner's comments

This is a thoughtful and considered response in which the text is explored and explained.

Retrieval

Answer the questions below. Cover the answers column with a piece of paper and write down as many as you can. Check and repeat.

	Questions	Answers
1	Give two negative descriptions of Scrooge from the early part of Stave I.	Two from: of 'tight-fisted' / 'grasping' / 'covetous old sinner'
2	Complete the quotation: '"His wealth is of no ___ ___ ___. He don't do any good with it. He don't make himself ___ with it."'	'"His wealth is of no use to him. He don't do any good with it. He don't make himself comfortable with it."'
3	What does Marley's Ghost reveal about the effect of his love of money when he lived?	It resulted in a miserable afterlife
4	What does Belle tell Scrooge his master passion has become?	'Gain'
5	Complete the quotation: '"in life my spirit never roved beyond the narrow limits of ___-___ ___ ___; and weary journeys lie before me!"'	'"in life my spirit never roved beyond the narrow limits of our money-changing hole; and weary journeys lie before me!"'
6	Complete the quotation using three words: '"it would be a bad fortune indeed to find so ___ _ ___ in his successor."'	'"it would be a bad fortune indeed to find so merciless a creditor in his successor."'
7	How do some of the businessmen in Stave IV display their wealth when they are in the city?	They 'chinked the money in their pockets […] and trifled thoughtfully with their great gold seals'
8	Dickens portrays the businessmen as having characteristics that a Victorian audience might have perceived as quite unpleasant. Name two of their physical attributes.	Two from: 'a great fat man' / 'monstrous chin' / 'red-faced' / 'with a pendulous excrescence on the end of his nose, that shook like the gills of a turkey-cock'
9	What themes are related to or contrasted with wealth, greed, and charity?	Poverty; the poor; social injustice
10	What ideas about money does Dickens promote?	Money should be used sensibly, shared, and given to charity

Put paper here

Previous questions

Now go back and use these questions to check your knowledge of previous topics.

	Questions	Answers
1	Which two words does Scrooge use to Fred in Stave I, to express his initial disgust about Christmas?	'"Bah!"'; "Humbug!"'
2	Who acts as the main mouthpiece for Dickens on the theme of Christmas?	Fred

Put paper here

Now turn to page 119 and complete Practice question 15.

20 Exam skills and sample answers

Exam skills

It is impossible to write a successful exam response unless you know the text thoroughly. Make sure you are familiar with the material on plot, method, characters, and themes.

REVISION TIP

There is a lot of printed and online advice about how to approach the exam. The best advice is contained in AQA's examiner reports, published on AQA's website, as these are written by the people who set papers and mark responses.

Key exam paper information

- There will be a single question on *A Christmas Carol* in Paper 1, Section B.
- You will spend roughly 50 minutes answering it.
- You will be given a question accompanied by bullet point reminders.
- There will be a printed extract that you must refer to in your response and you must also refer to the rest of the novel.
- You answer is marked out of 30.

Assessment objectives

Each question in Paper 1, Section B assesses AO1, AO2, and AO3:

- There are 12 marks available for AO1.
- There are 12 marks available for AO2.
- There are 6 marks available for AO3.

AO1: the quality of your response and understanding and use of the text

This includes the way you write, your use of vocabulary, and how you use references and quotations to show your understanding of the text.

The most important aspect of your writing is clarity of expression. You are expected to adopt a formal tone (not a chatty or casual one).

AO2: your understanding of the writer's methods

This means showing that you understand how the writer's language choice, form, and structure make meaning and create effects for the reader. You should use appropriate terms where needed.

Literary terms will only help you to gain marks if they are used correctly, and if they allow you to make a point clearly and precisely. There are no 'extra marks' for candidates who cram their answers with literary terminology for its own sake.

AO3: your understanding of ideas and contexts

This is about showing how well you understand the ideas and meanings in the text, and how they relate to the contexts in which they are written.

There is no need to write about historical context – often it gets in the way of a good answer. Writing about the ideas in the text, and the context of the characters in the story, is how you address AO3.

Types of questions

Questions on *A Christmas Carol* are always based on an extract, and are typically phrased in one of two ways:

> Starting with this extract, explore how Dickens presents ...

'explore' means you need to investigate and examine how Dickens presents the topic

or

> Starting with this extract, how does Dickens present ...

'how' means you need to show how Dickens presents the topic

Both types of question invite you to consider the various methods that Dickens uses to convey a specific theme or characteristic.

No matter which type of question you are given, remember that these questions give an opportunity to show off your knowledge of the text, its ideas, and the quality of your understanding.

A sample exam question

> Read the following extract from Chapter 1 of *A Christmas Carol* **1** and then answer the question that follows.
>
> In this extract, Scrooge speaks to Bob Cratchit before leaving the office to go home alone. **2**

1 This tells you where the extract comes from in the novel.

2 This reminds you of the context of the extract.

"You'll want all day to-morrow, I suppose?" said Scrooge.

"If quite convenient, sir."

"It's not convenient," said Scrooge, "and it's not fair. If I was to stop half-a-crown for it, you'd think yourself ill used, I'll be bound?"

3 The extract is usually between 15 and 35 lines.

The clerk smiled faintly.

"And yet," said Scrooge, "you don't think *me* ill used when I pay a day's wages for no work."

The clerk observed that it was only once a year.

"A poor excuse for picking a man's pocket every twenty-fifth of December!" said Scrooge, buttoning his great-coat to the chin. "But I suppose you must have the whole day. Be here all the earlier next morning."

The clerk promised that he would; and Scrooge walked out with a growl. The office was closed in a twinkling, and the clerk, with the long ends of his white comforter dangling below his waist (for he boasted no great-coat), went down a slide on Cornhill, at the end of a lane of boys, twenty

Knowledge EXAM SKILLS

20 Exam skills and sample answers

times, in honour of its being Christmas-eve, and then ran home to Camden Town as hard as he could pelt, to play at blindman's-buff.

Scrooge took his melancholy dinner in his usual melancholy tavern; and having read all the newspapers, and beguiled the rest of the evening with his banker's-book, went home to bed. He lived in chambers which had once belonged to his deceased partner.

They were a gloomy suite of rooms, in a lowering pile of building up a yard, where it had so little business to be, that one could scarcely help fancying it must have run there when it was a young house, playing at hide-and-seek with other houses, and have forgotten the way out again.

It was old enough now, and dreary enough; for nobody lived in it but Scrooge, the other rooms being all let out as offices. The yard was so dark that even Scrooge, who knew its every stone, was fain to grope with his hands.

The fog and frost so hung about the black old gateway of the house, that it seemed as if the Genius of the Weather sat in mournful meditation on the threshold.'

REMEMBER

The AOs are embedded in the question. This means that, if you answer the question, you are accessing the AOs naturally. You do not have to address the separate AOs individually; just make sure that your answer addresses both the bullet points

Starting with this extract (4), how does Dickens present (5) Scrooge as isolated in society? (6)

Write about:

- how Dickens presents Scrooge as isolated in society in this extract (7)
- how Dickens presents Scrooge as a isolated in society in the novel as a whole. (8)

(4) This reminds you to comment on the extract.

(5) This is an AO2 trigger, reminding you to focus on the writer's methods.

(6) This is the question focus – Scrooge as 'isolated'.

(7) This is a reminder to refer to Dickens' presentation of Scrooge in the extract.

(8) This is a reminder to refer to Dickens' presentation of Scrooge in the novel as a whole.

Planning and writing your response

Spend about 10 of the 50 minutes available by reading the extract carefully and jotting down notes to form a plan in your answer booklet.

1 Read the question (rather than the extract) and work out what you are being asked to do – underline key words.

2 Read the extract and underline anything relevant to the focus of the question.

3 List the points you will make in your answer – they must be relevant to the question.

4 Note down specific parts of the wider novel that are relevant to the question.

5 Begin your answer in a succinct way that directly addresses the focus of the question.

6 As you write your answer, support your points with references to precise points in the novel and/or with brief, relevant quotations.

7 In your conclusion, don't repeat points that you have made before, but refer back to the question focus.

EXAM TIP

Don't waste time by heavily annotating the extract – the examiner will never see this evidence of how perceptive you are!

EXAM TIP

You don't need to write a lot of pages to score highly, but you do need to write enough to show the quality of your understanding. Most successful answers are between three and four sides of the answer booklet.

How responses are assessed

Examiners read your answer in full and decide which level it is, awarding a mark out of 30. They will:

- decide how well you have kept your answer focused on the task in the question
- note your knowledge of plot, characters, language, themes, and meanings in *A Christmas Carol*, and how well you *use* that knowledge to answer the question
- reward your use of the text to support your answer, either through close reference to details of the plot, for example, or through short, purposeful quotations
- assess how well you understand and communicate the writer's methods in relation to the precise focus of the question.

REMEMBER

There is no direct link between the number of quotations you use and the mark you receive. It is possible to write an excellent response using only a few quotations or references, provided they support your ideas. Your ideas and your response to the precise focus of the question are what attract marks.

Knowledge EXAM SKILLS

20 Exam skills and sample answers

Mark scheme levels

Level 1: 1–5 marks	Level 2: 6–10 marks	Level 3: 11–16 marks
Simple, explicit comments	**Supported, relevant comments**	**Explained, structured comments**
• simple comments on text and task with a few relevant details • a little awareness of the writer making choices • possible reference to subject terminology • largely narrative or descriptive in approach • some simple reference to ideas/context	• supported reference to text and task • comments on references • identification of writer's methods • some reference to subject terminology • some awareness of implicit ideas/contextual factors	• some explained response to task and whole text • references used to support a range of relevant comments • relevant comments on writer's methods; relevant use of subject terminology • identification of effects of writer's methods to create meanings • some understanding shown by links between context/text/task

Level 4: 17–20 marks	Level 5: 21–25 marks	Level 6: 26–30 marks
Clear understanding	**Thoughtful, developed consideration**	**Convincing, critical analysis, and exploration**
• clear, explained response to task and whole text • effective use of references to support explanation • clear explanation of writer's methods; appropriate use of relevant subject terminology • understanding of effects of writer's methods to create meanings • clear understanding of ideas/contextual factors shown by specific links between context/text/task	• thoughtful, developed response to task and whole text • apt references integrated into interpretation • examination of writer's methods with effective subject terminology, supporting consideration of methods • examination of effects of writer's methods to create meanings • thoughtful consideration of ideas/contextual factors in detailed links between context/text/task	• critical, conceptualised response to task and whole text • judicious use of precise references to support interpretation(s) • analysis of writer's methods with subject terminology used judiciously • exploration of effects of writer's methods to create meanings • exploration of ideas/perspectives/contextual factors shown by specific, detailed links between context/text/task

Sample answer 1 – lower level

Here is an extract from a student response to the question on page 92, with the examiner's annotations and final comments. This response receives less than half marks.

In this extract, we see Scrooge go home alone 'with a growl', which suggests his bad temper. ❶ Scrooge eats his dinner in the same melancholy tavern every night and Christmas Eve, is no exception. ❷ Dickens tells us that he read the newspapers, and that he 'beguiled' himself with his 'banker's-book'. The word 'beguiled', suggests a charming activity which emphasises that Scrooge must be isolated to be so easily pleased with a 'banker's-book'. ❸ Elsewhere, Scrooge shows that he is isolated by refusing Fred's invitation to Christmas dinner. ❹ He tells the portly gentlemen 'I wish to be left alone', which appears to be something of a motto of his. ❺ In this extract, the isolated nature of Scrooge's home is highlighted by Dickens, describing it as 'a gloomy suite of rooms' standing alone, 'up a yard' – the description could almost be of 'gloomy' Scrooge himself, who keeps to himself. ❻ In Stave I, Dickens tells us directly that Scrooge is 'self-contained'. ❼ He describes him as the sort of person who even beggars avoided. He uses humour to stress this point by describing 'guide-dogs' for the blind tugging their owners 'into doorways' to escape Scrooge in his solitary walks around London. ❽

❶ 'Bad temper' may indicate someone who people don't wish to be with, but the candidate has not made that point.

❷ This implies a man of habit, but does not explicitly reference Scrooge's isolation.

❸ There is an attempt at the task here, and some attention to Dickens' use of language.

❹ Relevant point

❺ The quotation is useful; the idea about the motto is also useful, although we only hear Scrooge say this once.

❻ Fair point - could be developed

❼ Useful quotation to support

❽ Reference to Dickens' use of humour is a good 'method' point.

Examiner's comments

This response shows useful attention to the extract, as well as to Dickens' presentation of Scrooge as isolated elsewhere in Stave I. It could be improved by using a greater range of examples taken from across the novel.

Knowledge EXAM SKILLS

20 Exam skills and sample answers

Sample answer 2 – mid level

Here is a student response to the question on page 92, with the examiner's annotations and final comments. This response receives around half marks.

In this extract, Dickens presents Scrooge as isolated in a number of ways. ❶ He expects Bob to take less than a day's holiday for Christmas; revealing that he has no understanding of the significance of Christmas to families as he has no family of his own. ❷ He is so wedded to his solitary life that even when invited to Christmas dinner by his only relative – his nephew – he refuses. ❸ He carries his bad temper from arguing with Fred and meanly refusing to donate to charity into barking rudely at Bob, making him feel guilty for wanting 'all day'. ❹ Scrooge goes home to a 'gloomy suite of rooms' that used to belong to 'his deceased partner' – a reminder that Marley, whose 'only friend' was Scrooge, is dead. Dickens tells us that Scrooge was 'not so dreadfully cut up' by Marley's death so we see that friends don't mean much to Scrooge – probably because he prefers to be alone. ❺ Later, we see Scrooge has to 'grope with his hands' to find his way to his house, which is so dark that he cannot even see his way. We are told that 'nobody lived' in the house apart from Scrooge, implying a solitary life. Dickens uses the weather to reflect Scrooge's state of mind – 'fog and frost' hung about the 'gateway' to the house – reflecting Scrooge's cold character and his inability to recognise that his lonely existence is not what is expected in society. ❻ Previously, Scrooge calls the poor 'idle people', unworthy of his help. He pays taxes to 'support' prisons and workhouses,

❶ Immediate focus on the question

❷ A relevant point

❸ Factually accurate

❹ This point needs to be linked to the question more explicitly.

❺ Apt reference to another part of the text

❻ Text is used to suggest Scrooge's solitary life, and there is a reference to Dickens' use of language so thinks he has no further obligations to society but Marley's Ghost is about to change all that. 7 Later in the novel, Dickens shows how Scrooge came to be so isolated. The Ghost of Christmas Past shows Scrooge – and us – how he was left alone at Christmas (he 'wept to see his poor forgotten self') and how, when apprenticed, he had to sleep under a counter. These harsh lessons gave him a bitter outlook on others. He had a sister he loved but 'she died a woman', so Scrooge lost someone he loved and who loved him. 8 A similar loss occurs with Belle. Dickens tugs at our heart strings when Scrooge has to watch a 're-run' of his fiancée releasing him from his engagement, telling him he has found another 'idol' – 'Gain'. 9 Elsewhere, Dickens is emphatic about Scrooge's enjoyment of being alone, explaining that the 'very thing he liked' is 'To edge his way along the crowded paths of life, warning all human sympathy to keep its distance'. 10 Even the businessmen who worked alongside Scrooge are indifferent to news of his death. One of them says: 'I thought he'd never die'; while another who claims to be 'his most particular friend' is only prepared to attend his funeral if one of the others is going. 11 All in all, Dickens presents Scrooge as isolated but offers hope to the reader that any of us can change our course in life, if we take a close look at ourselves and rejoin and contribute to society. 12

7 Another apt reference to Dickens' presentation of Scrooge outside of the extract

8 The references to Scrooge's younger life are relevant; an unusual point about Scrooge's life as an apprentice, which is quite perceptive although this needs developing.

9 A text reference and the candidate identifies the methods mentioned so far as being plot-related

10 Useful quotation which would benefit from a further comment

11 These apt text references could be developed into a stronger point about the isolated figure that Scrooge has become.

12 A reasonable concluding paragraph, reminding the reader of the question focus

Examiner's comments

This response shows an understanding of some of Dickens' methods in presenting Scrooge as isolated in the extract, with some reference to the rest of the novel. There is some evidence of understanding how Dickens makes meaning. Links are made between the text and the question, focused text is used to support the answer.

REVISION TIP

Download an e-book for quick 'blasts of text' when you might normally just check your phone. Better still, get an audiobook of *A Christmas Carol* and listen to sections of it when you are doing other things.

20 Exam skills and sample answers

Sample answer 3 – higher level

Here is a student response to the question on page 92, with the examiner's annotations and final comments. This response receives high marks.

'You'll want all day to-morrow, I suppose?' said Scrooge. So starts the extract, with the voice of Scrooge himself. ❶ Dickens does not say how this rhetorical question was delivered. However, as readers, having heard Scrooge speak dismissively to his own nephew and tell the 'portly gentlemen' very rudely that he wishes 'to be left alone', we infer that his tone was harsh and his manner combative. In other words, the tone and manner of a man who is not inclined to be sociable, not even with own clerk, and not even on Christmas Eve. A truly isolated man. ❷ Scrooge selfishly begrudges Bob the 'whole' of Christmas day off work. A person who chooses to be isolated is selfish, as they do not wish to have to consider the needs or wishes of others. Scrooge makes Bob feel uncomfortable here by suggesting that he is the unreasonable one – in expecting to spend a day with his family – while Scrooge, with no family or friends to entertain him or to plague him, as Scrooge might see it, would have preferred another day in his 'counting house', counting out his money, perhaps, in front of a 'very small fire'. ❸ In Stave I, Dickens makes it plain to us that Scrooge is isolated. He tells us so directly introducing a powerful simile describing Scrooge as 'secret, and self-contained, and solitary as an oyster'. The idea of the oyster, locked inside its shell is a wonderfully vivid description of Scrooge. The 'shell' protects Scrooge from having to participate in the society that he cannot avoid being part of. Dickens makes us wonder if there

❶ This is a good start that immediately engages the reader's attention.

❷ An intelligent paragraph that sets the context of the printed extract and signals understanding.

❸ Although this is a little discursive, the candidate reflects on the isolation that Scrooge's character demonstrates; brief quotations support the ideas.

may be a pearl locked away within this oyster that might be revealed later in the story. ❹ Scrooge displays his self-imposed isolation so convincingly, when out-of-doors, that Dickens tells us that his outward appearance acts as a repellent to any casual enquirer after the time of day or street directions. ❺ Dickens uses humour, to help us appreciate Scrooge's demeanour, so unwelcoming that 'even the blind men's dogs' pulled their master out of Scrooge's way into 'doorways' when they see him coming, letting the man with the 'evil eye', go past them. ❻ Back in the extract, ❼ Scrooge grumbles to Bob, and to himself, about having his 'pocket picked' leaving Bob, 'with a growl', signifying his displeasure. In the society of the time, the employer had all the rights – the employee had none. Bob is ever fearful of losing his job which is why he tolerates his appalling working conditions (no fire to speak of) and unreasonable expectations about when he works. Dickens uses Bob as a foil to Scrooge to emphasise his isolation. Bob enjoys some companionable 'sliding' with a 'lane of boys' on his way home, while Scrooge 'took his melancholy dinner in his usual melancholy tavern' alone. ❽ For 'company', Scrooge has the newspapers and his 'banker's-book'. Dickens says that his banker's-book was able to 'beguile' him suggesting that, rather than take delight in the company of others, the loner, Scrooge, enjoys reminding himself of how much money he has accumulated. ❾ Dickens describes Scrooge's 'chambers' as 'gloomy', using pathetic fallacy to suggest that Scrooge, too, is gloomy by nature. This idea is extended further in the image of the building – stuck 'up a yard' like a 'young house' (or boy) forgotten during a game of 'hide and seek'. Dickens describes this as a 'fancy' or flight of the imagination. ❿

Continued

❹ Deft switch to looking at the wider novel; the quotation is commented upon in an interesting way

❺ Concise summary of Dickens' lengthier paragraph on Scrooge's behaviour to others

❻ Comment on Dickens' use of humour is apt

❼ The candidate moves easily between focus on the extract and on the wider text.

❽ Another method of Dickens is noted – using Bob as a foil to Scrooge – a well-selected moment

❾ Reference to text with useful comment and reference to isolation

❿ The candidate engages with Dickens' method of pathetic fallacy here and makes intelligent inferences.

The reader remembers it, however, when, in Stave II, the Spirit of Christmas Past shows Scrooge as 'a lonely boy' abandoned over Christmas and 'reading near a feeble fire'. To add to the pathos, Dickens describes the older Scrooge's reaction to this vision of his younger self: 'Scrooge sat down upon a form, and wept'. 11 This image of Scrooge, as a lonely, vulnerable child draws the reader's sympathy as does a later vision in the same stave, when Belle releases him from their engagement. Dickens uses a very short sentence to emphasise Scrooge's loss – 'She left him, and they parted.' 12 Both of these incidents may be intended by Dickens to help account for his isolation, in the 'present'. They certainly serve to draw reader sympathy. 13 A less sympathetic verdict on Scrooge is delivered by his charwoman who imagines Scrooge 'gasping out' his last breath 'alone by himself' because he had 'frightened everyone away from him when he was alive'. Dickens uses the charwoman as a rather coarse 'mouthpiece' for his own verdict on Scrooge, driving home his message about the fate of those who isolate themselves from society to focus entirely on themselves. 14

11 Useful links made to the wider novel

12 Consistent focus on the question; another useful example from Stave II

13 Considers Dickens' purpose in including these 'incidents' from Scrooge's past

14 Quite an effective conclusion, offering Dickens' own view of Scrooge as filtered through the charwoman's cynical view of him

Examiner's comments

The candidate offers a convincing response to the question, combining critical analysis with intelligent exploration of the extract and the wider text. Precise references are used to support the candidate's interpretation of Scrooge as isolated. There is effective analysis of Dickens' methods, and some useful reference to context is made.

REVISION TIP

Try writing your own answer to this question without looking at the sample answers. Make a quick plan and give yourself 45 minutes to write your answer. After you have finished, try applying the mark scheme to your answer and award it a level.

Retrieval

20

Answer the questions below. Cover the answers column with a piece of paper and write down as many as you can. Check and repeat.

	Questions	Answers
1	In the examination, will you have a choice of questions on *A Christmas Carol*?	No – there will be one question on *A Christmas Carol*
2	How many marks are available for your answer on *A Christmas Carol*?	30 marks
3	How long do you have to read the extract, plan and then write your answer?	50 minutes (provided that you did not spend too long on your Shakespeare question)
4	Do I have to refer to external historical context in my answer?	No – there is no need to refer to external historial context, you need to show that you understand the setting and the context of characters in the story
5	Do I have to write about Dickens' life in my answer?	No
6	Is it worth memorising lots of long quotations to use in the exam?	No – a short, appropriate quotation will support your answer just as effectively
7	Do references to the text have to be exact quotations?	No – but if you keep your quotations short, you will usually get them right
8	Will references that are not quotations be credited?	Yes – if you clearly identify a specific place in the plot or in the development of a character, that is just as helpful as a quotation
9	You should make a plan on the answer booklet before writing the answer. True or false?	True
10	What sort of length of answer should you aim for in the exam?	Between three and four sides of the answer booklet

Put paper here

Previous questions

Now go back and use these questions to check your knowledge of previous topics.

	Questions	Answers
1	Name two motifs or images that Dickens uses to show Scrooge's progress.	Two from: light / dark / warmth / cold
2	Which of the three Ghosts of Christmas tells Scrooge that their business with him is his 'reclamation'?	The Ghost of Christmas Past

Put paper here

Practice

Exam-style questions

Use the questions in this section to practise the knowledge and skills you have learned.

1

Read the following extract from Chapter 1 (Stave I) of *A Christmas Carol* and then answer the question that follows.

In this extract, the reader is introduced to Scrooge for the first time.

Scrooge never painted out Old Marley's name. There it stood, years afterwards, above the warehouse door: Scrooge and Marley. The firm was known as Scrooge and Marley. Sometimes people new to the business called Scrooge Scrooge, and sometimes Marley, but he answered to both names. It was all the same to him.

Oh! But he was a tight-fisted hand at the grindstone, Scrooge! a squeezing, wrenching, grasping, scraping, clutching, covetous, old sinner! Hard and sharp as flint, from which no steel had ever struck out generous fire; secret, and self-contained, and solitary as an oyster. The cold within him froze his old features, nipped his pointed nose, shrivelled his cheek, stiffened his gait; made his eyes red, his thin lips blue; and spoke out shrewdly in his grating voice. A frosty rime was on his head, and on his eyebrows, and his wiry chin. He carried his own low temperature always about with him; he iced his office in the dog-days; and didn't thaw it one degree at Christmas.

External heat and cold had little influence on Scrooge. No warmth could warm, no wintry weather chill him. No wind that blew was bitterer than he, no falling snow was more intent upon its purpose, no pelting rain less open to entreaty. Foul weather didn't know where to have him. The heaviest rain, and snow, and hail, and sleet, could boast of the advantage over him in only one respect. They often "came down" handsomely, and Scrooge never did.

Nobody ever stopped him in the street to say, with gladsome looks, "My dear Scrooge, how are you? When will you come to see me?" No beggars implored him to bestow a trifle, no children asked him what it was o'clock, no man or woman ever once in all his life inquired the way to such and such a place, of Scrooge. Even the blind men's dogs appeared to know him; and when they saw him coming on, would tug their owners into doorways and up courts; and then would wag their tails as though they said, "No eye at all is better than an evil eye, dark master!"

Starting with this extract, explore how Dickens presents the character of Scrooge in *A Christmas Carol*.

Write about:

- how Dickens presents Scrooge in this extract
- how Dickens presents Scrooge in the novel as a whole.

[30 marks]

EXAM TIP

Remember to begin by planning an answer. Start your thinking by looking at the question first rather than the extract.

2

Read the following extract from Chapter 1 (Stave I) of *A Christmas Carol* and then answer the question that follows.

In this extract, the reader is introduced to Fred for the first time.

"Christmas a humbug, uncle!" said Scrooge's nephew. "You don't mean that, I am sure?"

"I do," said Scrooge. "Merry Christmas! What right have you to be merry? What reason have you to be merry? You're poor enough."

"Come, then," returned the nephew gaily. "What right have you to be dismal? What reason have you to be morose? You're rich enough."

Scrooge, having no better answer ready on the spur of the moment, said, "Bah!" again; and followed it up with "Humbug."

"Don't be cross, uncle!" said the nephew.

"What else can I be," returned the uncle, "when I live in such a world of fools as this? Merry Christmas! Out upon merry Christmas! What's Christmas time to you but a time for paying bills without money; a time for finding yourself a year older, and not an hour richer; a time for balancing your books, and having every item in 'em through a round dozen of months presented dead against you? If I could work my will," said Scrooge indignantly, "every idiot who goes about with 'Merry Christmas' on his lips should be boiled with his own pudding, and buried with a stake of holly through his heart. He should!"

"Uncle!" pleaded the nephew.

"Nephew!" returned the uncle sternly, "keep Christmas in your own way, and let me keep it in mine."

"Keep it!" repeated Scrooge's nephew. "But you don't keep it."

"Let me leave it alone, then," said Scrooge. "Much good may it do you! Much good it has ever done you!"

"There are many things from which I might have derived good, by which I have not profited, I dare say," returned the nephew. "Christmas among the rest. But I am sure I have always thought of Christmas time, when it has come round—apart from the veneration due to its sacred name and origin, if anything belonging to it can be apart from that—as a good time; a kind, forgiving, charitable, pleasant time; the only time I know of, in the long calendar of

Continued

EXAM TIP

Don't be put off if the extract is one you are less familiar with. Remember that it is the question that is most important, so look for parts of the extract that link directly to the question and start with those.

Practice

Exam-style questions

the year, when men and women seem by one consent to open their shut-up hearts freely, and to think of people below them as if they really were fellow-passengers to the grave, and not another race of creatures bound on other journeys. And therefore, uncle, though it has never put a scrap of gold or silver in my pocket, I believe that it *has* done me good, and *will* do me good; and I say, God bless it!"

Starting with this extract, explore how Dickens presents Fred as a sympathetic character in *A Christmas Carol*.

Write about:

- how Dickens presents Fred sympathetically in this extract
- how Dickens presents Fred sympathetically in the novel as a whole.

[30 marks]

3

Read the following extract from Chapter 1 (Stave I) of *A Christmas Carol* and then answer the question that follows.

In this extract, Scrooge sees Marley's Ghost.

"I cannot rest, I cannot stay, I cannot linger anywhere. My spirit never walked beyond our counting-house—mark me!—in life my spirit never roved beyond the narrow limits of our money-changing hole; and weary journeys lie before me!"

It was a habit with Scrooge, whenever he became thoughtful, to put his hands in his breeches pockets. Pondering on what the Ghost had said, he did so now, but without lifting up his eyes, or getting off his knees.

"You must have been very slow about it, Jacob," Scrooge observed in a business-like manner, though with humility and deference.

"Slow!" the Ghost repeated.

"Seven years dead," mused Scrooge. "And travelling all the time!"

"The whole time," said the Ghost. "No rest, no peace. Incessant torture of remorse."

"You travel fast?" said Scrooge.

"On the wings of the wind," replied the Ghost.

"You might have got over a great quantity of ground in seven years," said Scrooge.

The Ghost, on hearing this, set up another cry, and clanked its chain so hideously in the dead silence of the night, that the Ward would have been justified in indicting it for a nuisance.

"Oh! captive, bound, and double-ironed," cried the phantom, "not to know, that ages of incessant labour, by immortal creatures, for this earth must pass into eternity before the good of which it is susceptible is all developed. Not to know that any Christian spirit working kindly in its little sphere, whatever it may be, will find its mortal life too short for its vast means of usefulness. Not to know that no space of regret can make amends for one life's opportunities misused! Yet such was I! Oh! such was I!"

"But you were always a good man of business, Jacob," faltered Scrooge, who now began to apply this to himself.

"Business!" cried the Ghost, wringing its hands again. "Mankind was my business. The common welfare was my business; charity, mercy, forbearance, and benevolence were, all, my business. The dealings of my trade were but a drop of water in the comprehensive ocean of my business!"

Starting with this extract, explore how Dickens presents the idea that charity and kindness are more important in life than making money in *A Christmas Carol*.

Write about:

- how Dickens presents this idea about charity and benevolence in this extract
- how Dickens presents this idea about charity and benevolence in the novel as a whole.

[30 marks]

EXAM TIP

Questions are likely to refer to chapters rather than staves but they will be referring to same the section of the story.

Practice

Exam-style questions

4

Read the following extract from Chapter 3 (Stave III) of *A Christmas Carol* and then answer the question that follows.

In this extract, Scrooge first observes the Cratchit family on Christmas Day.

Martha didn't like to see him disappointed, if it were only in joke; so she came out prematurely from behind the closet door, and ran into his arms, while the two young Cratchits hustled Tiny Tim, and bore him off into the wash-house, that he might hear the pudding singing in the copper.

"And how did little Tim behave?" asked Mrs. Cratchit when she had rallied Bob on his credulity, and Bob had hugged his daughter to his heart's content.

"As good as gold," said Bob, "and better. Somehow he gets thoughtful, sitting by himself so much, and thinks the strangest things you ever heard. He told me, coming home, that he hoped the people saw him in the church, because he was a cripple, and it might be pleasant to them to remember upon Christmas Day who made lame beggars walk, and blind men see."

Bob's voice was tremulous when he told them this, and trembled more when he said that Tiny Tim was growing strong and hearty.

His active little crutch was heard upon the floor, and back came Tiny Tim before another word was spoken, escorted by his brother and sister to his stool beside the fire; and while Bob, turning up his cuffs—as if, poor fellow, they were capable of being made more shabby—compounded some hot mixture in a jug with gin and lemons, and stirred it round and round and put it on the hob to simmer; Master Peter and the two ubiquitous young Cratchits went to fetch the goose, with which they soon returned in high procession.

Such a bustle ensued that you might have thought a goose the rarest of all birds; a feathered phenomenon, to which a black swan was a matter of course—and in truth it was something very like it in that house. Mrs. Cratchit made the gravy (ready beforehand in a little saucepan) hissing hot; Master Peter mashed the potatoes with incredible vigour; Miss Belinda sweetened up the apple-sauce; Martha dusted the hot plates; Bob took Tiny Tim beside him in a tiny corner at the table; the two young Cratchits set chairs for everybody, not forgetting themselves, and mounting guard upon their posts, crammed spoons into their mouths, lest they should shriek for goose before their turn came to be helped. At last the dishes were set on, and grace was said. It was succeeded by a breathless pause, as Mrs. Cratchit, looking slowly all along the carving-knife, prepared to plunge it in the breast; but when she did, and when the long-expected gush of stuffing issued forth, one murmur of delight arose all round the board, and even Tiny Tim, excited by the two young Cratchits, beat on the table with the handle of his knife, and feebly cried Hurrah!

Starting with this extract, explore how Dickens presents the Cratchit family in *A Christmas Carol*.

Write about:

- how Dickens presents the Cratchit family in this extract
- how Dickens presents the Cratchit family in the novel as a whole.

[30 marks]

5

Read the following extract from Chapter 2 (Stave II) of *A Christmas Carol* and then answer the question that follows.

In this extract, Scrooge has reluctantly watched Belle with her family.

And now Scrooge looked on more attentively than ever, when the master of the house, having his daughter leaning fondly on him, sat down with her and her mother at his own fireside; and when he thought that such another creature, quite as graceful and as full of promise, might have called him father, and been a spring-time in the haggard winter of his life, his sight grew very dim indeed.

"Belle," said the husband, turning to his wife with a smile, "I saw an old friend of yours this afternoon."

"Who was it?"

"Guess!"

"How can I? Tut, don't I know?" she added in the same breath, laughing as he laughed. "Mr. Scrooge."

"Mr. Scrooge it was. I passed his office window; and as it was not shut up, and he had a candle inside, I could scarcely help seeing him. His partner lies upon the point of death, I hear; and there he sat alone. Quite alone in the world, I do believe."

"Spirit!" said Scrooge in a broken voice, "remove me from this place."

"I told you these were shadows of the things that have been," said the Ghost. "That they are what they are, do not blame me!"

"Remove me!" Scrooge exclaimed. "I cannot bear it!"

He turned upon the Ghost, and seeing that it looked upon him with a face in which in some strange way there were fragments of all the faces it had shown him, wrestled with it. "Leave me! Take me back! Haunt me no longer!"

In the struggle, if that can be called a struggle in which the Ghost with no visible resistance on its own part was undisturbed by any effort of its adversary, Scrooge observed that its light was burning high and bright; and dimly connecting that with its influence over him, he seized the extinguisher-cap, and by a sudden action pressed it down upon its head.

Practice

Exam-style questions

Starting with this extract, explore how Dickens presents Scrooge's regrets about his past behaviour in *A Christmas Carol*.

Write about:

- how Dickens presents Scrooge's regrets about his past behaviour in this extract
- how Dickens presents regret in the novel as a whole.

[30 marks]

EXAM TIP

When selecting parts from the extract to use in your answer, always make sure the lines you choose are directly relevant to the question being asked.

6

Read the following extract from Chapter 5 (Stave V) of *A Christmas Carol* and then answer the question that follows.

In this extract, Scrooge reveals to Bob his plans to start helping him and his family straight away.

But he was early at the office next morning. Oh, he was early there! If he could only be there first, and catch Bob Cratchit coming late! That was the thing he had set his heart upon.

And he did it; yes, he did! The clock struck nine. No Bob. A quarter past. No Bob. He was full eighteen minutes and a half behind his time. Scrooge sat with his door wide open, that he might see him come into the Tank.

His hat was off before he opened the door; his comforter too. He was on his stool in a jiffy; driving away with his pen, as if he were trying to overtake nine o'clock.

"Hallo!" growled Scrooge, in his accustomed voice, as near as he could feign it. "What do you mean by coming here at this time of day?"

"I am very sorry, sir," said Bob. "I *am* behind my time."

"You are?" repeated Scrooge. "Yes. I think you are. Step this way, sir, if you please."

"It's only once a year, sir," pleaded Bob, appearing from the Tank. "It shall not be repeated. I was making rather merry yesterday, sir."

"Now, I'll tell you what, my friend," said Scrooge. "I am not going to stand this sort of thing any longer. And therefore," he continued, leaping from his stool, and giving Bob such a dig in the waistcoat that he staggered back into the Tank again: "and therefore I am about to raise your salary!"

EXAM TIP

When planning an answer, you might find that there are lots of points you could make. Choose the most impressive ideas and write about those in detail, rather than trying to cover every point.

Bob trembled, and got a little nearer to the ruler. He had a momentary idea of knocking Scrooge down with it, holding him, and calling to the people in the court for help and a strait-waistcoat.

"A merry Christmas, Bob!" said Scrooge, with an earnestness that could not be mistaken, as he clapped him on the back. "A merrier Christmas, Bob, my good fellow, than I have given you for many a year! I'll raise your salary, and endeavour to assist your struggling family, and we will discuss your affairs this very afternoon, over a Christmas bowl of smoking bishop, Bob! Make up the fires and buy another coal-scuttle before you dot another i, Bob Cratchit!"

Starting with this extract, explore how Dickens presents the relationship between Scrooge and Bob Cratchit in *A Christmas Carol*.

Write about:

- how Dickens presents the relationship between Scrooge and Bob Cratchit in this extract
- how Dickens presents the relationship between Scrooge and Bob Cratchit in the novel as a whole.

[30 marks]

7

Read the following extract from Chapter 2 (Stave II) of *A Christmas Carol* and then answer the question that follows.

In this extract, the Ghost of Christmas Past takes Scrooge back to his school.

"One Christmas time, when yonder solitary child was left here all alone, he *did* come, for the first time, just like that. Poor boy! And Valentine," said Scrooge, "and his wild brother, Orson; there they go! And what's his name, who was put down in his drawers, asleep, at the gate of Damascus; don't you see him! And the Sultan's Groom turned upside down by the Genii: there he is upon his head! Serve him right. I'm glad of it. What business had *he* to be married to the Princess?"

To hear Scrooge expending all the earnestness of his nature on such subjects, in a most extraordinary voice between laughing and crying; and to see his heightened and excited face; would have been a surprise to his business friends in the City, indeed.

Continued

Practice

Exam-style questions

"There's the Parrot!" cried Scrooge. "Green body and yellow tail, with a thing like a lettuce growing out of the top of his head; there he is! Poor Robin Crusoe, he called him, when he came home again after sailing round the island. 'Poor Robin Crusoe, where have you been, Robin Crusoe?' The man thought he was dreaming, but he wasn't. It was the Parrot, you know. There goes Friday, running for his life to the little creek! Halloa! Hoop! Halloo!"

Then, with a rapidity of transition very foreign to his usual character, he said, in pity for his former self, "Poor boy!" and cried again.

"I wish," Scrooge muttered, putting his hand in his pocket, and looking about him, after drying his eyes with his cuff: "but it's too late now."

"What is the matter?" asked the Spirit.

"Nothing," said Scrooge. "Nothing. There was a boy singing a Christmas Carol at my door last night. I should like to have given him something: that's all."

The Ghost smiled thoughtfully, and waved its hand: saying, as it did so, "Let us see another Christmas!"

Starting with this extract, explore how Dickens presents Scrooge as a character who changes.

Write about:

- how Dickens presents Scrooge's emotions in this extract
- how Dickens presents change in the novel as a whole.

[30 marks]

8

Read the following extract from Chapter 5 (Stave V) of *A Christmas Carol* and then answer the question that follows.

In this extract, Scrooge wakes up on Christmas morning after seeing the Ghost of Christmas Yet to Come.

YES! and the bedpost was his own. The bed was his own, the room was his own. Best and happiest of all, the Time before him was his own, to make amends in!

"I will live in the Past, the Present, and the Future!" Scrooge repeated as he scrambled out of bed. "The Spirits of all Three shall strive within me. Oh, Jacob Marley! Heaven and the Christmas Time be praised for this! I say it on my knees, old Jacob; on my knees!"

He was so fluttered and so glowing with his good intentions, that his broken voice would scarcely answer to his call. He had been sobbing violently in his conflict with the Spirit, and his face was wet with tears.

"They are not torn down," cried Scrooge, folding one of his bed-curtains in his arms, "they are not torn down, rings and all. They are here—I am here—the shadows of the things that would have been may be dispelled. They will be. I know they will!"

His hands were busy with his garments all this time; turning them inside out, putting them on upside down, tearing them, mislaying them, making them parties to every kind of extravagance.

"I don't know what to do!" cried Scrooge, laughing and crying in the same breath; and making a perfect Laocoön of himself with his stockings. "I am as light as a feather, I am as happy as an angel, I am as merry as a schoolboy. I am as giddy as a drunken man. A merry Christmas to everybody! A happy New Year to all the world! Hallo here! Whoop! Hallo!"

He had frisked into the sitting-room, and was now standing there: perfectly winded.

"There's the saucepan that the gruel was in!" cried Scrooge, starting off again, and going round the fire-place. "There's the door by which the Ghost of Jacob Marley entered! There's the corner where the Ghost of Christmas Present, sat! There's the window where I saw the wandering Spirits! It's all right, it's all true, it all happened. Ha, ha, ha!"

Starting with this extract, explore how Dickens presents the theme of time in *A Christmas Carol*.

Write about:

- how Dickens presents the theme of time in this extract
- how Dickens presents the theme of time in the novel as a whole.

[30 marks]

EXAM TIP

Remember to focus your answer on the big ideas and themes that relate to the question. Always try to write in detail and show the quality of your thinking in relation to the idea in the question.

Practice

Exam-style questions

9

Read the following extract from Chapter 2 (Stave II) of *A Christmas Carol* and then answer the question that follows.

In this extract, the Ghost of Christmas Past shows Scrooge the Christmas party he attended at Mr Fezziwig's warehouse when he was a young man.

Old Fezziwig laid down his pen, and looked up at the clock, which pointed to the hour of seven. He rubbed his hands; adjusted his capacious waistcoat; laughed all over himself, from his shoes to his organ of benevolence, and called out in a comfortable, oily, rich, fat, jovial voice:

"Yo ho, there! Ebenezer! Dick!"

Scrooge's former self, now grown a young man, came briskly in, accompanied by his fellow-'prentice.

"Dick Wilkins, to be sure!" said Scrooge to the Ghost. "Bless me, yes. There he is. He was very much attached to me, was Dick. Poor Dick! Dear, dear!"

"Yo ho, my boys!" said Fezziwig. "No more work to-night. Christmas Eve, Dick. Christmas, Ebenezer! Let's have the shutters up," cried old Fezziwig with a sharp clap of his hands, "before a man can say Jack Robinson!"

You wouldn't believe how those two fellows went at it! They charged into the street with the shutters—one, two, three—had 'em up in their places—four, five, six—barred 'em and pinned 'em—seven, eight, nine—and came back before you could have got to twelve, panting like race-horses.

"Hilli-ho!" cried old Fezziwig, skipping down from the high desk, with wonderful agility. "Clear away, my lads, and let's have lots of room here! Hilli-ho, Dick! Chirrup, Ebenezer!"

Clear away! There was nothing they wouldn't have cleared away, or couldn't have cleared away, with old Fezziwig looking on. It was done in a minute. Every movable was packed off, as if it were dismissed from public life for evermore; the floor was swept and watered, the lamps were trimmed, fuel was heaped upon the fire; and the warehouse was as snug, and warm, and dry, and bright a ball-room, as you would desire to see upon a winter's night.

In came a fiddler with a music-book, and went up to the lofty desk, and made an orchestra of it, and tuned like fifty stomach-aches. In came Mrs. Fezziwig, one vast substantial smile. In came the three Miss Fezziwigs, beaming and lovable. In came the six young followers whose hearts they broke. In came all the young men and women employed in the business.

Starting with this extract, explore how Dickens presents the theme of the Christmas spirit in *A Christmas Carol*.

Write about:

- how Dickens presents the theme of the Christmas spirit in this extract
- how Dickens presents the theme of the Christmas spirit in the novel as a whole.

[30 marks]

EXAM TIP

Look closely at the way each question is set up. Remember that 'how far' questions require a judgement on your part.

10

Read the following extract from Chapter 3 (Stave III) of *A Christmas Carol* and then answer the question that follows.

In this extract, Bob Cratchit's family celebrate Christmas, watched by Scrooge and the Ghost of Christmas Present.

"If these shadows remain unaltered by the Future, none other of my race," returned the Ghost, "will find him here. What then? If he be like to die, he had better do it, and decrease the surplus population."

Scrooge hung his head to hear his own words quoted by the Spirit, and was overcome with penitence and grief.

"Man," said the Ghost, "if man you be in heart, not adamant, forbear that wicked cant until you have discovered What the surplus is, and Where it is. Will you decide what men shall live, what men shall die? It may be that, in the sight of Heaven, you are more worthless and less fit to live than millions like this poor man's child. Oh God! to hear the Insect on the leaf pronouncing on the too much life among his hungry brothers in the dust!"

Scrooge bent before the Ghost's rebuke, and trembling cast his eyes upon the ground. But he raised them speedily, on hearing his own name.

"Mr. Scrooge!" said Bob. "I'll give you Mr. Scrooge, the Founder of the Feast!"

"The Founder of the Feast indeed!" cried Mrs. Cratchit, reddening. "I wish I had him here. I'd give him a piece of my mind to feast upon, and I hope he'd have a good appetite for it."

"My dear," said Bob, "the children! Christmas Day."

"It should be Christmas Day, I am sure," said she, "on which one drinks the health of such an odious, stingy, hard, unfeeling man as Mr. Scrooge. You know he is, Robert! Nobody knows it better than you do, poor fellow!"

"My dear!" was Bob's mild answer, "Christmas Day."

Continued

Practice

Exam-style questions

"I'll drink his health for your sake and the Day's," said Mrs. Cratchit, "not for his. Long life to him! A merry Christmas and a happy new year! He'll be very merry and very happy, I have no doubt!"

The children drank the toast after her. It was the first of their proceedings which had no heartiness. Tiny Tim drank it last of all, but he didn't care twopence for it. Scrooge was the Ogre of the family. The mention of his name cast a dark shadow on the party, which was not dispelled for full five minutes.

Starting with this extract, explore how Dickens shows the character of Scrooge in *A Christmas Carol*.

Write about:

- how Dickens presents the character of Scrooge in this extract
- how Dickens presents the character of Scrooge in the novel as a whole.

[30 marks]

11

Read the following extract from Chapter 4 (Stave IV) of *A Christmas Carol* and then answer the question that follows.

In this extract, Mrs Cratchit and her family prepare for Tiny Tim's funeral.

The mother laid her work upon the table, and put her hand up to her face.

"The colour hurts my eyes," she said.

The colour? Ah, poor Tiny Tim!

"They're better now again," said Cratchit's wife. "It makes them weak by candlelight; and I wouldn't show weak eyes to your father when he comes home, for the world. It must be near his time."

"Past it rather," Peter answered, shutting up his book. "But I think he has walked a little slower than he used, these few last evenings, mother."

They were very quiet again. At last she said, and in a steady, cheerful voice, that only faltered once:

"I have known him walk with—I have known him walk with Tiny Tim upon his shoulder, very fast indeed."

"And so have I," cried Peter. "Often."

"And so have I," exclaimed another. So had all.

"But he was very light to carry," she resumed, intent upon her work, "and his father loved him so, that it was no trouble: no trouble. And there is your father at the door!"

She hurried out to meet him; and little Bob in his comforter—he had need of it, poor fellow—came in. His tea was ready for him on the hob, and they all tried who should help him to it most. Then the two young Cratchits got upon his knees and laid, each child a little cheek, against his face, as if they said, "Don't mind it, father. Don't be grieved!"

Bob was very cheerful with them, and spoke pleasantly to all the family. He looked at the work upon the table, and praised the industry and speed of Mrs. Cratchit and the girls. They would be done long before Sunday, he said.

"Sunday! You went to-day, then, Robert?" said his wife.

"Yes, my dear," returned Bob. "I wish you could have gone. It would have done you good to see how green a place it is. But you'll see it often. I promised him that I would walk there on a Sunday. My little, little child!" cried Bob. "My little child!"

Starting with this extract, explore how Dickens presents the Cratchits in *A Christmas Carol*.

Write about:

- how Dickens presents the Cratchits in this extract
- how Dickens presents the Cratchits in the novel as a whole.

[30 marks]

EXAM TIP

When answering questions that focus on more than one character, there is no need to write about all of them equally, but make sure that you do cover more than one.

12

Read the following extract from Chapter 4 (Stave IV) of *A Christmas Carol* and then answer the question that follows.

In this extract, the Ghost of Christmas Yet to Come shows Scrooge how news of his death is received by people who owe him money.

The Phantom spread its dark robe before him for a moment, like a wing; and withdrawing it, revealed a room by daylight, where a mother and her children were.

She was expecting some one, and with anxious eagerness; for she walked up and down the room; started at every sound; looked out from the window; glanced at the clock; tried, but in vain, to work with her needle; and could hardly bear the voices of the children in their play.

Continued

Practice

Exam-style questions

At length the long-expected knock was heard. She hurried to the door, and met her husband; a man whose face was careworn and depressed, though he was young. There was a remarkable expression in it now; a kind of serious delight of which he felt ashamed, and which he struggled to repress.

He sat down to the dinner that had been hoarding for him by the fire; and when she asked him faintly what news (which was not until after a long silence), he appeared embarrassed how to answer.

"Is it good," she said, "or bad?" —to help him.

"Bad," he answered.

"We are quite ruined?"

"No. There is hope yet, Caroline."

"If *he* relents," she said, amazed, "there is! Nothing is past hope, if such a miracle has happened."

"He is past relenting," said her husband. "He is dead."

She was a mild and patient creature if her face spoke truth; but she was thankful in her soul to hear it, and she said so, with clasped hands. She prayed forgiveness the next moment, and was sorry; but the first was the emotion of her heart.

"What the half-drunken woman whom I told you of last night, said to me, when I tried to see him and obtain a week's delay; and what I thought was a mere excuse to avoid me; turns out to have been quite true. He was not only very ill, but dying, then."

"To whom will our debt be transferred?"

"I don't know. But before that time we shall be ready with the money; and even though we were not, it would be bad fortune indeed to find so merciless a creditor in his successor. We may sleep to-night with light hearts, Caroline!"

Starting with this extract, explore how Dickens creates tension in *A Christmas Carol*.

Write about:

- how Dickens creates tension in this extract
- how Dickens creates tension in the novel as a whole.

[30 marks]

EXAM TIP

Start your answer with a brief outline of your overall argument or point of view. Then use the rest of your answer to develop and support this.

13

Read the following extract from Chapter 3 (Stave III) of *A Christmas Carol* and then answer the question that follows.

In this extract, Fred's Christmas party is watched by the Ghost of Christmas Present and Scrooge.

"His wealth is of no use to him. He don't do any good with it. He don't make himself comfortable with it. He hasn't the satisfaction of thinking—ha, ha, ha!—that he is ever going to benefit US with it."

"I have no patience with him," observed Scrooge's niece. Scrooge's niece's sisters, and all the other ladies, expressed the same opinion.

"Oh, I have!" said Scrooge's nephew. "I am sorry for him; I couldn't be angry with him if I tried. Who suffers by his ill whims? Himself, always. Here, he takes it into his head to dislike us, and he won't come and dine with us. What's the consequence? He don't lose much of a dinner."

"Indeed, I think he loses a very good dinner," interrupted Scrooge's niece. Everybody else said the same, and they must be allowed to have been competent judges, because they had just had dinner; and, with the dessert upon the table, were clustered round the fire, by lamplight.

"Well! I'm very glad to hear it," said Scrooge's nephew, "because I haven't any great faith in these young housekeepers. What do *you* say, Topper?"

Topper had clearly got his eye upon one of Scrooge's niece's sisters, for he answered that a bachelor was a wretched outcast, who had no right to express an opinion on the subject. Whereat Scrooge's niece's sister—the plump one with the lace tucker: not the one with the roses—blushed.

"Do go on, Fred," said Scrooge's niece, clapping her hands. "He never finishes what he begins to say! He is such a ridiculous fellow!"

Scrooge's nephew revelled in another laugh, and as it was impossible to keep the infection off; though the plump sister tried hard to do it with aromatic vinegar; his example was unanimously followed.

"I was only going to say," said Scrooge's nephew, "that the consequences of his taking a dislike to us, and not making merry with us, is, as I think, that he loses some pleasant moments, which could do him no harm. I am sure he loses pleasanter companions than he can find in his own thoughts, either in his mouldy old office, or his dusty chambers. I mean to give him the same chance every year, whether he likes it or not, for I pity him. He may rail at Christmas till he dies, but he can't help thinking better of it—I defy him—if he finds me going there, in good temper, year after year, and saying, Uncle Scrooge, how are you?"

Practice

Exam-style questions

Starting with this extract, explore how Dickens presents the theme of family in *A Christmas Carol*.

Write about:

- how Dickens presents the theme of family in this extract
- how Dickens presents the theme of family in the novel as a whole.

[30 marks]

EXAM TIP

The AOs are embedded in the question. This means that if you answer the question, you are accessing the AOs naturally. Rather than consciously trying to 'do' AOs, just answer the question.

14

Read the following extract from Chapter 5 (Stave V) of *A Christmas Carol* and then answer the question that follows.

In this extract, Scrooge is enjoying Christmas, going out into the streets and to Fred's Christmas dinner.

He dressed himself "all in his best," and at last got out into the streets. The people were by this time pouring forth, as he had seen them with the Ghost of Christmas Present; and walking with his hands behind him, Scrooge regarded every one with a delighted smile. He looked so irresistibly pleasant, in a word, that three or four good-humoured fellows said, "Good morning, sir! A merry Christmas to you!" And Scrooge said often afterwards that, of all the blithe sounds he had ever heard, those were the blithest in his ears.

He had not gone far, when coming on towards him he beheld the portly gentleman, who had walked into his counting-house the day before, and said, "Scrooge and Marley's, I believe?" It sent a pang across his heart to think how this old gentleman would look upon him when they met; but he knew what path lay straight before him, and he took it.

"My dear sir," said Scrooge, quickening his pace, and taking the old gentleman by both his hands. "How do you do? I hope you succeeded yesterday. It was very kind of you. A merry Christmas to you, sir!"

"Mr. Scrooge?"

"Yes," said Scrooge. "That is my name, and I fear it may not be pleasant to you. Allow me to ask your pardon. And will you have the goodness"—here Scrooge whispered in his ear.

"Lord bless me!" cried the gentleman, as if his breath were taken away. "My dear Mr. Scrooge, are you serious?"

"If you please," said Scrooge. "Not a farthing less. A great many back-payments are included in it, I assure you. Will you do me that favour?"

"My dear sir," said the other, shaking hands with him. "I don't know what to say to such munifi—"

"Don't say anything, please," retorted Scrooge. "Come and see me. Will you come and see me?"

"I will!" cried the old gentleman. And it was clear he meant to do it.

"Thank'ee," said Scrooge. "I am much obliged to you. I thank you fifty times. Bless you!"

He went to church, and walked about the streets, and watched the people hurrying to and fro, and patted children on the head, and questioned beggars, and looked down into the kitchens of houses, and up to the windows, and found that everything could yield him pleasure. He had never dreamed that any walk—that anything—could give him so much happiness. In the afternoon he turned his steps towards his nephew's house.

He passed the door a dozen times before he had the courage to go up and knock. But he made a dash, and did it.

Starting with this extract, explore how Dickens presents the theme of redemption in *A Christmas Carol*.

Write about:

- how Dickens presents the theme of redemption in this extract
- how Dickens presents the theme of redemption in the novel as a whole.

[30 marks]

EXAM TIP

Remember that the key term in a question has a variety of synonyms and these can help you develop ideas. For example, a question about redemption should prompt you to think about reclamation, salvation, and enlightenment.

15

Read the following extract from Chapter 1 (Stave I) of *A Christmas Carol* and then answer the question that follows.

The extract shows Scrooge refusing to donate money to help the poor at Christmas.

They were portly gentlemen, pleasant to behold, and now stood, with their hats off, in Scrooge's office. They had books and papers in their hands, and bowed to him.

"Scrooge and Marley's, I believe," said one of the gentlemen, referring to his list. "Have I the pleasure of addressing Mr. Scrooge, or Mr. Marley?"

Continued

Practice

Exam-style questions

"Mr. Marley has been dead these seven years," Scrooge replied. "He died seven years ago, this very night."

"We have no doubt his liberality is well represented by his surviving partner," said the gentleman, presenting his credentials.

It certainly was; for they had been two kindred spirits. At the ominous word "liberality" Scrooge frowned, and shook his head, and handed the credentials back.

"At this festive season of the year, Mr. Scrooge," said the gentleman, taking up a pen, "it is more than usually desirable that we should make some slight provision for the poor and destitute, who suffer greatly at the present time. Many thousands are in want of common necessaries; hundreds of thousands are in want of common comforts, sir."

"Are there no prisons?" asked Scrooge.

"Plenty of prisons," said the gentleman, laying down the pen again.

"And the Union workhouses?" demanded Scrooge. "Are they still in operation?"

"They are. Still," returned the gentleman, "I wish I could say they were not."

"The Treadmill and the Poor Law are in full vigour, then?" said Scrooge.

"Both very busy, sir."

"Oh! I was afraid, from what you said at first, that something had occurred to stop them in their useful course," said Scrooge. "I'm very glad to hear it."

"Under the impression that they scarcely furnish Christian cheer of mind or body to the multitude," returned the gentleman, "a few of us are endeavouring to raise a fund to buy the Poor some meat and drink, and means of warmth. We choose this time, because it is a time, of all others, when Want is keenly felt, and Abundance rejoices. What shall I put you down for?"

"Nothing!" Scrooge replied.

Starting with this extract, explore how Dickens presents attitudes towards the poor in *A Christmas Carol*.

Write about:

- how Dickens presents attitudes towards the poor in this extract
- how Dickens presents attitudes towards the poor in the novel as a whole.

[30 marks]

16

Read the following extract from the end of Chapter 3 (Stave III) of *A Christmas Carol* and then answer the question that follows.

In this extract, the Ghost of Christmas Present shows Scrooge two children.

"Forgive me if I am not justified in what I ask," said Scrooge, looking intently at the Spirit's robe, "but I see something strange, and not belonging to yourself, protruding from your skirts. Is it a foot or a claw?"

"It might be a claw, for the flesh there is upon it," was the Spirit's sorrowful reply. "Look here."

From the foldings of its robe it brought two children; wretched, abject, frightful, hideous, miserable. They knelt down at its feet, and clung upon the outside of its garment.

"Oh, Man! look here! Look, look, down here!" exclaimed the Ghost.

They were a boy and girl. Yellow, meagre, ragged, scowling, wolfish; but prostrate, too, in their humility. Where graceful youth should have filled their features out, and touched them with its freshest tints, a stale and shrivelled hand, like that of age, had pinched, and twisted them, and pulled them into shreds. Where angels might have sat enthroned, devils lurked, and glared out menacing. No change, no degradation, no perversion of humanity, in any grade, through all the mysteries of wonderful creation, has monsters half so horrible and dread.

Scrooge started back, appalled. Having them shown to him in this way, he tried to say they were fine children, but the words choked themselves, rather than be parties to a lie of such enormous magnitude.

"Spirit! are they yours?" Scrooge could say no more.

"They are Man's," said the Spirit, looking down upon them. "And they cling to me, appealing from their fathers. This boy is Ignorance. This girl is Want. Beware of them both, and all of their degree, but most of all beware this boy, for on his brow I see that written which is Doom, unless the writing be erased. Deny it!" cried the Spirit, stretching out its hand towards the city. "Slander those who tell it ye! Admit it for your factious purposes, and make it worse! And bide the end!"

"Have they no refuge or resource?" cried Scrooge.

"Are there no prisons?" said the Spirit, turning on him for the last time with his own words. "Are there no workhouses?"

The bell struck twelve.

Practice

Exam-style questions

Starting with this extract, explore how Dickens presents poverty in *A Christmas Carol*.

Write about:

- how Dickens presents poverty in this extract
- how Dickens presents poverty in the novel as a whole.

[30 marks]

EXAM TIP

You do not need to refer to complex techniques and terms to do well. It is your point or interpretation that is important.

17

Read the following extract from Chapter 3 (Stave III) of *A Christmas Carol* and then answer the question that follows.

In this extract, the Cratchit family have Christmas dinner, watched by Scrooge and the Ghost of Christmas Present.

"God bless us every one!" said Tiny Tim, the last of all.

He sat very close to his father's side, upon his little stool. Bob held his withered little hand in his, as if he loved the child, and wished to keep him by his side, and dreaded that he might be taken from him.

"Spirit," said Scrooge with an interest he had never felt before, "tell me if Tiny Tim will live."

"I see a vacant seat," replied the Ghost, "in the poor chimney-corner, and a crutch without an owner, carefully preserved. If these shadows remain unaltered by the Future, the child will die."

"No, no," said Scrooge. "Oh, no, kind Spirit! say he will be spared."

"If these shadows remain unaltered by the Future, none other of my race," returned the Ghost, "will find him here. What then? If he be like to die, he had better do it, and decrease the surplus population."

Scrooge hung his head to hear his own words quoted by the Spirit, and was overcome with penitence and grief.

"Man," said the Ghost, "if man you be in heart, not adamant, forbear that wicked cant until you have discovered What the surplus is, and Where it is. Will you decide what men shall live, what men shall die? It may be, that in the sight of Heaven, you are more worthless and less fit to live than millions like this poor man's child. Oh God! to hear the Insect on the leaf pronouncing on the too much life among his hungry brothers in the dust!"

Scrooge bent before the Ghost's rebuke, and trembling cast his eyes upon the ground. But he raised them speedily, on hearing his own name.

"Mr. Scrooge!" said Bob. "I'll give you Mr. Scrooge, the Founder of the Feast!"

"The Founder of the Feast, indeed!" cried Mrs. Cratchit, reddening. "I wish I had him here. I'd give him a piece of my mind to feast upon, and I hope he'd have a good appetite for it."

"My dear," said Bob, "the children! Christmas Day."

Starting with this extract, explore how Dickens presents Tiny Tim in *A Christmas Carol*.

Write about:

- how Dickens presents Tiny Tim in this extract
- how Dickens presents Tiny Tim in the novel as a whole.

[30 marks]

OXFORD
UNIVERSITY PRESS

Great Clarendon Street, Oxford, OX2 6DP, United Kingdom

Oxford University Press is a department of the University of Oxford. It furthers the University's objective of excellence in research, scholarship, and education by publishing worldwide. Oxford is a registered trademark of Oxford University Press in the UK and in certain other countries.

Series Editor: Lyndsay Bawden

Written by Su Fielder

First published in 2025

British Library Cataloguing in Publication Data

Data available

978-1-382-06746-1

978-1-382-06745-4 (ebook)

10 9 8 7 6 5 4 3 2 1

The manufacturing process conforms to the environmental regulations of the country of origin.

Printed in the UK by Bell & Bain.

The manufacturer's authorised representative in the EU for product safety is Oxford University Press España S.A. of el Parque Empresarial San Fernando de Henares, Avenida de Castilla, 2 – 28850 Madrid (www.oup.es/en or product.safety@oup.com). OUP España S.A. also acts as importer into Spain of products made by the manufacturer.

Acknowledgements

The publisher would like to thank Jade Hickin and Sarah Cottinghatt for sharing their expertise and feedback in the development of this resource.

Extracts are from *Essential Student Texts: A Christmas Carol* (Oxford University Press, 2020)

Although we have made every effort to trace and contact all copyright holders before publication this has not been possible in all cases. If notified, the publisher will rectify any errors or omissions at the earliest opportunity.

FSC
www.fsc.org
MIX
Paper | Supporting responsible forestry
FSC® C007785